Ugo Betti

Ugo Betti

An Introduction

by

Emanuele Licastro

McFarland & Company, Inc., Publishers
Jefferson, North Carolina, and London

Also by Emanuele Licastro:
Luigi Pirandello, dalle novelle alle commedie
(Verona, Fiorini, 1974)

Frontispiece: Peter Michael Goetz and Coleen
Dewhurst in *Queen and the Rebels*. Photograph
© 1983 by Martha Swope, New York City.

Library of Congress Cataloging in Publication Data

Licastro, Emanuele.
  Ugo Betti.

  Bibliography: p.
  Includes index.
    1. Betti, Ugo, 1892–1953 — Criticism and inter-
pretation. I. Title.
PQ4807.E85Z64 1985   852'.912   84-43202

ISBN 0-89950-141-9 (alk. paper)

Printed in the United States of America.

McFarland   Box 611   Jefferson NC 28640

To my parents,
Rosa Maddaloni Licastro and Francesco Licastro

Contents

Acknowledgments

I am grateful to Martin Pops for reading my manuscript and for offering suggestions toward its improvement. I should like to thank Cappelli Publishers for permission to quote from Betti's *Teatro completo*. I wish to thank Mrs. Charline Zent for her help in typing the final manuscript.

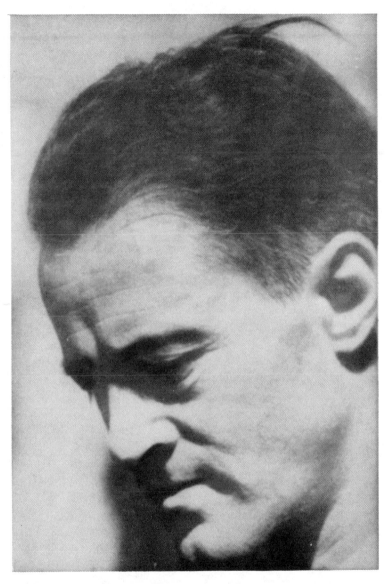

Ugo Betti. (Photograph is of unknown date.)

Preface

"No artist ... can feel comfortable as a Christian; every artist who happens also to be a Christian wishes he could be a polytheist" — so writes W.H. Auden.[1] Ugo Betti is a playwright in apparent struggle with his Christianity: the impermanence, dislocation, doubt, questioning, probing, pain, anguish, terror, absurdity, and nihilism that we find in his most arresting pages tell us clearly that his artistic world is far from a sphere of blessedness. Indeed his most significant plays seem to take place in hell and only in hell. While Dante's *iter* goes from the darkest pits through the nostalgic and hopeful purgatorial ledges to the most splendid heavenly light, Betti, a son of the twentieth century, seems never to grasp a moment of steadfast certitude or even of positive expectancy.

The most positive moments are those which breathe the faint and incipient hope of a better world, and these moments are rare. For Betti inexorably drives his characters to a never-ending search within themselves and leaves them nakedly questioning. His theater is epistemological not ontological. His inquests, the most common form of his plays, are vain quests for truth, authenticity. Yet in the background, far back, there seem to be some flickerings of light, of meaning and goodness. For Betti[2] believes that even the most callous criminal has a remnant of

xi

humanity—or at least the wish for it. It would be, then, more appropriate to think of Betti as struggling with his humanity— what he called "that weighty crown above our heads: conscious- ness"[3]—rather than with his Christianity, as Saint Augustine does, or Dante or Michelangelo.

Betti's best plays hypnotize the reader and the spectator with apocalyptic questions—Who am I? Why am I as I am? Why is the world? Why is the world as it is? Betti was always pursued by devils he could not leave behind; his last play is characteristically entitled *La fuggitiva* (*The Fugitive*). Betti transforms these con- cerns—it is their transformation, after all, which makes him the artist he is—into a theatrical language, at times melodic, lyrical, dream-like, fantastic; at other times coarse, terse, frightened, cacophonic, and jazz-like. And he is an artist in his original use of stagecraft: characters sometimes speak their intimate thoughts only to themselves and the audience, characters are sometimes seen by only one other player and the audience, the dead some- times come alive on stage. These are among the devices which bring to life and—most of all—to powerful realization what Betti wants to express and communicate. One wouldn't immediately suspect, as one critic rightly observes, that "Betti may be de- scribed as a dramatist in the classic manner [and that] his plays are technically among the best of our century, and made on solid traditional lines."[4]

This is the first book in English on Ugo Betti, an introduc- tion, and I have chosen the most straightforward and clearest approach to his work. Instead of selecting Betti's best or most representative works and building on them—with reference to the others—a comprehensive view of the author, I have chosen instead to consider his *oeuvre* itself—facilitated in this by its not overwhelming size—in the hope that the view will be more complete. For the sake of this completeness I have noticed, however briefly, even the very minor works.

Emanuele Licastro
Buffalo, N.Y. January 1984

Chronology

Milan on October 3. In September he marries; he is transferred as a judge to Rome.

1931   The collection *Canzonette — La morte* (*Little Songs — Death*) wins the Mondadori poetry prize.

1932   *Un Albergo sul porto* (*An Inn on the Harbor*) is chosen as the best play at the *Concorso Drammatico Nazionale* by the Governatorato di Roma. He finishes *Frana allo Scalo Nord* (*Landslide at the North Station*).

1933   He polemicizes against the *rondisti* and is a contributor to *Oggi*.

1936   Composition of *Una bella domenica di settembre (A Beautiful September Sunday)*. Première of *Frana allo Scalo Nord*.

1939   The script *I tre del Pra' di Sopra* (*The Three Men from the Meadow*) wins a contest set up by the magazine *Cinema*.

1941   Composition of *Il vento notturno* (*The Night Wind*).

1945   He finishes *Corruzione al Palazzo di Giustizia* (*Corruption in the Palace of Justice*).

1946   In January he finishes *Ispezione* (*The Inquiry*). Composition of *Delitto all'Isola delle Capre (Crime on Goat Island)*.

1949   *Corruption in the Palace of Justice* wins first prize awarded by the *Istituto del Dramma Italiano*, as the best play of the season 1948–1949 for theater. (The prize for poetry goes to Ungaretti, for film to Rossellini.) Composition of *La Regina e gli insorti* (*The Queen and the Rebels*). On September 14, *Lotta fino all'alba* (*Struggle Till Dawn*) opens in Paris.

1950   On October 20, *Crime on Goat Island* opens in Rome.

1953   He completes *La fuggitiva* (*The Fugitive*). On April 23, *Crime on Goat Island* opens in Paris. On June 9, Betti dies.

Sin is not so much knowing...as wanting to know
(*Albert Camus*, The Myth of Sisyphus).

Chapter 1

Betti's Life

Ugo Betti's outward biography adds little to the understanding of his inner biography. Nor has his intellectual biography — his contact with the intelligentsia of his time and place — much bearing on the playwright; for his aesthetic acts cannot be linked to any literary trend or figure. Although his father, Tullio, kept a journal about him until he was in his thirties — Betti was born in Camerino on February 4, 1892 — we don't find in it "the portrait of the artist as a young man," the process of spiritual maturation and growth of the future writer.

Because of his father's "excessive and fanatic" love — as he confesses in the journal — there remain Betti's first verse (even a poem when he was eight), and compositions which show an ordinary enough pattern for an intelligent young man studying literature and the classics. In his teens he imitated the poets he was studying: first Alfieri and Foscolo, then Carducci, Pascoli, and the *crepuscolari* poets. He also did translations from the Latin, and his translation of Catullus' *Epithalamion of Thetis and Peleus* was published with his father's financial help in 1910. In his prose juvenilia young Betti didn't follow any one current or master, and he wrote mostly of social and moral themes. On one such theme he built a juvenile play about a prostitute who, not being able to change her life, kills herself. By the end of his

1

university years Betti was influenced by the cultural milieu of the Italian Marches, the province most attracted by extreme socialism and social revolution, and he adopted the futurist mask of sarcasm to lash the idiocy of the bourgeoisie. His doctoral dissertation, *Il diritto e la rivoluzione* (1914; *Law and Revolution*) sings the praises of revolutionary behavior which will correct the injustices of society and give dignity to the individual. Betti reveals a familiarity with the ideas of Marx, Sorel, Max Stirner, and Nietzsche.

In 1915, convinced that intervention in the war would be the best way of bringing about socialism in Italy, Betti volunteered and from spring 1916 he was in combat until taken prisoner in October 1917 during the defeat at Caporetto. In his last battle he distinguished himself for bravery and was decorated. He remained a prisoner, first in Rastatt, then in Cellelager, until the end of 1918.

War and prison experience changed Betti's attitudes, and the verses he composed at the front and in prison show a different writer from the one of his university years. The melancholic and nostalgic dreams and fables he now wrote are the heart of his first book, *Il re pensieroso* (1922; *The Pensive King*), but what is more revealing is how Betti's intellectual interests widen. He requests from the front and from prison books by Serao, Deledda, Moretti, Gozzano, Pascoli, Rosso di San Secondo; by non-Italian authors, Tolstoy, Dostoyevsky, Turgenev, Shakespeare, Ibsen, Chekhov, Poe, Wilde, Verlaine, Maeterlinck, Baudelaire, Mallarmé and Rimbaud.

After the war Betti began his lifelong career in the magistrature: first in Parma until 1930, the year of his marriage to Andreina Frosini, then as a judge in Rome. He had already written a book of short stories, *Caino*, published in 1928, and, more important, he had composed his first drama, *La padrona* (*The Mistress of the House*), in 1924, which won first prize offered by the theater magazine, *Le scimmie e lo specchio*, in 1925. *La padrona* was performed that year and received warmly by the critics, coldly by the public.

Although he continued to write short stories—his last collection *Una strana serata* (*A Strange Evening*) came out in

1948 — and although he published a novel (also in 1948), and several movie scripts before and after the Second World War, by the late 1920's Betti had discovered his true vocation as a dramatist. By 1930 he had already written three more theater pieces — *La casa sull'acqua* (*The House on the Water*), *Un albergo sul porto* (*An Inn on the Harbor*) and *L'isola meravigliosa* (*The Marvelous Island*) — the last of which won a prize in a contest by the Governatorato di Roma in July 1930. In 1932 Betti finished the play we may call his first masterpiece, *Frana allo Scalo Nord* (*Landslide at the North Station*).

The years 1932 and 1933 were the only time in his life when Betti was active as a public literary figure. In the controversy between *veristi* and *rondisti* — the former defended the view that art should be interested in life's actual concerns while the *rondisti* (from the title of a literary magazine, *La ronda* [*The Patrol*] published from 1919 to 1923) championed an art of stylistic refinement, of the beautiful page, of the exceptional fragment — Betti was the most outspoken of the *veristi*, the first and most frequent contributor to the Fascist[1] "weekly of letters and arts," *Oggi*, published in Rome from May 21 to December 31, 1933. Other contributors were Tilgher, Brancati, Cecchi, Moravia, Jovine.[2] None of these writers displayed much political sympathy for Fascism, especially for what it was to become. As for Betti himself, his politics were such that in 1938 he was accused of being an antifascist and a Jew.

In 1941, Betti started what one of his translators, the poet Henry Reed, thought "must be among the greatest outbursts in dramatic literature."[3] From then until his death he composed thirteen plays, among them the best of his *oeuvre*, on the same level of achievement as *Landslide*. His fame had gathered by 1947; by 1950 some thought him Italy's greatest living playwright. In 1949, with *Corruzione al Palazzo di Giustizia* (*Corruption in the Palace of Justice*), Betti had his first clamorous success with an Italian audience, though during his lifetime, his native success was never complete or unanimous. Outside Italy, toward the end, his plays were enthusiastically received. On his deathbed, he heard that *Delitto all'Isola delle Capre* (*Crime on Goat Island*) was being acclaimed in Paris.

With the comforting rituals of Christianity, whose practice he had not attended since his teens, Betti died on June 9, 1953. The consensus was growing that, after Pirandello, he was Italy's greatest modern playwright.

Chapter 2

Suffering and Self-Knowledge
(1924–1934)

We would like at least…to understand why life
is the marvelous tranquil iniquity that it is
(Ugo Betti, Preface to The Mistress of the House).

In the Preface to his very first play, *La padrona* (1924), Ugo Betti writes in a disarmingly straightforward, and disingenuous fashion that "every human act appears absolutely obvious and petty if one considers its outer shell, but it seems to become little by little an entirely different matter when our thought enters its tortuous roots which are soon swallowed by the shadow."[1] This statement in its simplicity epitomizes Betti's theater, for most of his plays are a search into the human heart.

Betti's most peculiarly theatrical devices are the return to the scene of action of a person known to the other characters; the coming of a stranger; and the trial or inspection. These three devices resolve themselves into an inquest; into a reversal of a personal or interpersonal situation; or into an uncovering of inauthenticity in characters hidden behind a mask of pity, self-pity, fear, rhetoric, or sheer malice. The inquest into the "tortuous roots" of some characters' behavior and feelings becomes a quest into

5

shadows which brings forth by the end of the play a new situation revealing guilt, desire for atonement, longing for purity, faith in the Christian God, or an unconscious incestuous desire. Thus many of Betti's characters are stripped of the armor with which they defend themselves from others and hide from themselves; they stand alone, "naked" in their authenticity, and with an unbearable self-knowledge.

I. La padrona

La padrona (*The Mistress of the House*) has the appearance of an old-fashioned realistic drama, but the language, lyrical and suggestive, derails the action into a fable of life against death.

It is spring and young Anna, sick with tuberculosis, comes back from the sanatorium to her family's two-room house. Her old father, Pietro, has just taken a new wife, Marina, a much younger woman who is filled with an almost animal vitality. She is the new, absolute mistress of the house in spite of the fact that Pietro claims he is the master ("Who is the master?"[2]), and Anna claims she is mistress of her life ("I am still the mistress.")[3] though death is gnawing at her.

But it is Marina who dominates. She despises Pietro who, in his old age, is "bewitched"[4] by the overpowering beauty and warmth of his wife; it is almost as if he could become young again near her. Anna also feels an irresistible attraction for Marina ("I have fallen in love with you! I think about you at night even! I dream of you...."[5]), as if she wanted to regain her health near her who is so healthy.

In the second act Marina, now pregnant, asks Pietro to sell his shoemaker shop and to send away the sickly Anna so that her presence won't contaminate her child. Pietro, who cannot resign himself to the injustice of the world, asks himself about cosmic responsibility ("But then, whose fault is it?"[6]), is convinced that in the universe "there is something that clashes...,"[7] and that many human beings live "like fish out of water."[8] Feeling proud of his future heir, he is full of hope and is about to send away his daughter when she reveals to him that he is not the real father.

The third act starts after the funeral of the baby. Its death is almost the realization of Anna's desire, as if she doesn't want others to live if she cannot. It appears also as Marina's wish fulfillment — she had also said: "It could die"[9] — as if she wanted to eliminate any possible obstacle to her freedom. The agon is between the life instincts, beautiful in their exuberance, innocent in their cruelty, and the lack of vitality represented by the drunken old man and by death, imminent in the form of fatal illness.

The play consists of two main movements towards life: the first is symbolized by springtime at the outset and the hope for Anna's recovery; the other is symbolized by Marina's pregnancy with which Act II begins. Both movements fail. At the beginning of Act III the spectators learn of the death of the baby, which is a premonition of Anna's death. It seems it was Betti's intention to underline this struggle when he originally entitled the play *Life and Death*.

At the end, life, represented by Marina, prevails. She decides to go away in spite of the fact that Pietro tells her she can do anything she wants if she stays, and that she is mistress. Anna, an image of death, becomes more and more mad with envy the more she feels death approaching. Marina had told her: "You are like someone who is drowning and would like...to pull down the sun with him!"[10] Anna succeeds in undoing her father's last scruples and convinces him to kill her stepmother, but when Pietro is about to kill Marina, he is stopped by the dying Anna's last scream. With her last breath she asks her father to let Marina go: "The door...open the door for her...."[11]

Instinctual drives and the desire for happiness live on, indifferent to the injustice of the world; sorrow doesn't have any meaning, human or religious; it is an unexplainable and unavoidable datum. The world completely lacks that "harmony" of which Betti speaks in the Preface to this drama. Betti's universe, at the beginning of his theatrical career, is enveloped in a close and suffocating atmosphere. One of the minor characters of *The Mistress of the House* refers to Anna, Marina, and Pietro in the following way: "You are three, locked in here biting one another, and the taste of blood makes you drunk...."[12] Which seems a preview of Sartre's hell in *Closed Door*. There is neither the attempt at an *askesis* towards a life of justice, peace and love, nor a *discensus* into that underworld of the human soul full of monsters. Not one of the characters seems near the possibility of redemption. Even Pietro, who is the least monolithic, the least unidimensional, "is indeed suffering but still is confused...there isn't a yet well-defined consciousness of guilt."[13]

It is this unidimensional aspect of the characters which limits the play. Yet one can notice several elements which will be developed in later works. The most obvious is the coming of a character from afar who will have the function of a catalyst: here it is Il parente who comes from America and remains on the stage for almost the entire first act; he is the one who challenges the characters to know themselves and to reveal themselves to each other and to the audience; but he remains extraneous to the plot and he seems a mere *deus ex machina* meant to start, not to solve, the action.

II. La casa sull'acqua

A more integral part of the plot and of greater consequence is the outsider who comes at the beginning of Betti's second play, *La casa sull'acqua* (1928; *The House on the Water*). Elli succeeds in awakening the characters from a resigned life devoid of any interest or eagerness. The brothers Francesco and Luca have forgotten the desires and dreams of their adolescence and youth: Francesco was thinking of travelling and even of becoming an admiral; Luca had ambitions of becoming a painter. They live with Marta, Francesco's wife and owner of a house near a lake whose waters reach beneath the house, to a dock where the family used to keep boats during the winter.

Water is one among several motifs Betti uses symbolically in the *oeuvre*—others are desert, wind, mountain, port, station, and, of course, tribunal. The conception and the image of the house on the water succeeds in rescuing the play from a superficial realism; this haunting and peculiar setting suggests an ideal, enchanted, almost surreal atmosphere. Another twist which forces our attention out of a commonplace frame of mind is the

paradox of water not as life-giving but as stagnant, which en-
forces a lifelessness upon the inhabitants of the house—Marta's
barrenness is the most obvious aspect of it. But even more arid
are the souls of the two brothers. Francesco and Luca lead a life
of mechanical routine, they seem to mark time, ready to die if not
to commit suicide. The situation is intriguing since the two
brothers appear entirely different in their physique and in their
character. Francesco is a strong and big man who takes care of
the property, likes hunting and chases after the women workers;
he dominates his wife and brother, his wife through love, his
brother through fear and envy. Luca, on the other hand, is weak
and sickly, he owns no property, is not interested in working or in
anything else. He lives off his brother's and his sister-in-law's
charity and wears his brother's old clothes. He has forgotten he
was an architect and his pleasure in painting.

When the outsider, Elli, a childhood friend, comes from
America to sell her property, the brothers seem to awaken. (Elli is
diminutive of Felicita, and the suggestion of the sun is not casual;
the most devastating Bettian outsider is called Angelo in *Goat
Island*). Elli throws light in the darkness of their situation; her
warmth generates the beginning of hope. This play doesn't take
the form of inquest or trial, yet Elli foreshadows the inquisitors
and the investigators of later plays. Soon after she steps onto the
stage, she asks about Francesco: "What does he do? Does he get
bored?"[14] To Luca, as soon as she recognizes him, her first question is: "What do you do?"[15] and then pursues with: "How old
are you?" And after Luca says he is not working or painting, she
relentlessly, almost cruelly, adds: "But perhaps you are getting
bored!"[16] Later, after asserting that she wants to be happy, she
seems to bring them to the breaking point of despair with the
most cruel question of all: "And what about you? Are you
happy?[17] Luca's answer—or non-answer—is the most poignant
line in the play: "I carve pieces of wood."[18] It could be an answer
of an idiot or a child. In fact, his wood carving of small animals is
the only vestige of that artistic talent which he now realizes could
have led him to happiness in his life. Now that Elli has opened his
eyes, he longingly recalls when he first discovered that talent: "It
was as if I had opened a little door: life before me was, I don't

know...a marvelous garden."[19] But he has to conclude that he has lost that garden: "The key to that little door, to that garden... I'd lost it!"[20] In spite of his weakness and passivity, Luca is able to confront dialectically the disturbing question (Are you happy? — I am not. I could have been). The strong, feared, and active Francesco doesn't even have an answer. While Luca's reaction belongs within a non-heroic psychological framework — Why am I unhappy? How could I be happy? — Francesco's confrontation of the problem of happiness is posited within a heroic, perhaps heroically anti-heroic, metaphysical vision, which doesn't allow the consideration itself of the problem, let alone a possible solution. Instead of answering, he speaks of useless toil, pointing out that whatever one does, one will end up in the cemetery. He is keenly aware of the passage of time, and to Elli's insistence on asking about "intentions, hopes," he is speechless; he can only laugh. Yet he also, like his brother, desperately grasps for the change represented by Elli. But while Luca, who has already started to paint again, makes an effort, sensing a doubt or hope that men are created for an end other than just suffering, Francesco scorns the possibility of any aim and "violently" asks: "And why did God, if He exists, create us so full of poison,...sheep and wolves?"[21] He wants to act according to the law of the jungle and of the survival of the fittest. With his strength and brutality he wants to possess Elli, feeling, almost in spite of himself, an obscure desire for change. He is taking her from Luca who, because of her, and with her, is about to start a new life, again enthusiastic about painting and excited with the preparations of the paper lanterns for the yearly feast, something he used to do when he was very young. Afraid, Luca literally begs Francesco on his knees, but Francesco answers that he also has nothing. Luca asks for pity and Francesco answers "*sobbing*: 'Luca, it is I who ask pity from you!... Be compassionate.... Don't you see that I am like you, unhappier than you, hopeless, old...'"[22] and finally: "Kill me, I will be happy!"[23] In the middle of this exchange they hear that the rotten wood in another part of the house has given way and that Elli, who was running from the brothers, has fallen in the water. Believing her dead, Francesco confesses: "It is my fault. Forgive me."[24]

The final moment of decision arrives when the servant announces that the young lady is still alive. Francesco is the one who can and must choose between taking Elli or not. His is not the conventional choice of the desperate man (the one Luca would have made), but the one of a man beyond desperation, of a man aware that no matter what, anguish befalls him forever. He renounces a futile attempt at happiness (Felicita means happiness) and leaves Elli to his brother. "You go, Luca. You go,"[25] he says as the play ends.

During the play one sometimes has the impression that Francesco may be a poseur, but his last act makes him a lonely and sincere figure; one of those Dantean sinners who don't ask for compassion. He is one of the most existential Bettian creatures in his awareness and acceptance of his unredeemable guilt and anguish.

III. L'isola meravigliosa

Sometimes, lyricism becomes an artistic limitation in Ugo Betti's theater: not lyricism per se but its overuse in situations whose main import is of a more realistic and speculative bent. Betti uses it always at face value, so to speak. In fact, one cannot point out a single instance in which lyricism is made use of with dialectical intention as a mere theatrical value, as, for example, in the famous Pirandellian instance in *Six Characters in Search of an Author*, when the Stepdaughter describes the scene in the garden with her small sister. Pirandello means that lyrical description *also* as a mockery of the sentimentalized, true-to-life, bourgeois theater, to which the greater part of his audience was accustomed, the drama to be performed — *la commedia da fare* — as against the real performed drama. However, Betti's next play is a successful lyrical work.

Although in his youthful verses, he rarely achieves poetical purity, Betti has a genuine lyrical vein; but he is more engaging when he endeavors to combine it with drama which is, after all, where his talent as an artist really lies. *L'isola meravigliosa* (1929; *The Marvelous Island*) is not in verse form but its language is chosen mainly for its poetic power rather than its communicative or colloquial utility. In this work Betti is interested in the shaping of images, suggesting moments of intensity of feeling, recalling to the surface archetypal sensations, fears, longings. The play is a drama which takes the form of a tale. It is based on the old-age popular wisdom and belief that it is humanly impossible to be happy; no one can achieve happiness, no matter how many possessions; even a king can be unhappy. Betti's fable tells that even a king *must* be unhappy.

Nadir is a king thought demented because he keeps on travelling, on questing without rest. On his ships he goes from island to island—some curse is on him as it is on other wandering or flying legendary figures. He is forever searching, never reaching, "happy lands"; always on the run, "forgetting that happiness runs faster than anyone."[26] He has come now, for a short rest, to "the marvelous island" which Anfis, the royal doctor, calls "the gem of the whole domain," full of every attraction and "fertilized with the dead." They all try to convince the king to stop wandering and to stay, to be officially crowned. The mayor of the island offers him a scepter and riches—but Nadir commands and owns anything he wants. He offers wisdom and the king rejects it. He offers a special balm to cure every sickness—"except old age," Anfis adds. The mayor then offers the beauty of a rose which blooms every nine hundred years but which, Anfis adds, will last but a morning. This image recalls some verses of Malherbe's poem *Consolation à M. Du Périer*: "Et Rose elle a vescu ce que vivent les Roses, / L'espace d'un matin."[27] (And Rose, she lived as long as Roses live, for only a morning.) One cannot be sure, but perhaps it is a spontaneous recollection on Betti's part, for in Act I, scene iii, after quoting some lines by Rilke he goes to the trouble of footnoting the author. At another point there is a clear reference, not footnoted, to Foscolo's *I Sepolcri*, and there are intimations (perhaps unconscious) of the *Fioretti di San Francesco*. All this shouldn't be taken as pedantism but as evidence of the poetic inspiration of the play.

Since lyricism is Betti's main interest, the play takes the form of almost obligatory scenes which are only a pretext for the expression of various sensations or sentiments. In fact, not one of the mayor's gifts—the last two being a beautiful girl and a liquor of which one drop can induce the most pleasurable dreams, but two will kill—can make Nadir happy. He is searching for "what is, what lasts, what is true"[28]; and since happiness [*letizia*] "either it is within us or in no place,"[29] nothing that is or can be given has the power of making Nadir or anyone else happy.

Although tired of travelling, the king refuses to remain in "the marvelous island." Anfis decides to "fabricate" for him a dream-like life with the help of the magician Sparamosca, who casts a spell and convinces Nadir that what he needs to be happy, Sparamosca, like God, can make out of nothing. Nadir finally is happy with what the magician has created: the enchanting maiden, Maidune, whose name means "the one everyone wants and nobody can find,"[30] that is, happiness. Nadir ends his wandering and stays on the island.

In the second act, Nadir refuses to be crowned. The patriarch thinks he will accept the crown from Maidune, but the king still rejects it; Maidune, in love and desperation, reveals her real identity, she is just a poor girl. The spell is broken, and Sparamosca screams: "a fable is ended. Open your eyes: mad king!"[31] Nadir in pain and anger has the magician blinded and gives Maidune to a beggar.

In the third act, because of a rebellion, the king and his cousin, Bima, both disguised, are trying to reach a sailing ship. They meet a group of beggars—a hunchback, a lame man, a one-handed man, a one-eyed man—but when the two are about to leave, a woman's voice is heard singing the same song Maidune used to sing. The king, enchanted, asks of the woman, "tattered and withered," where she learned the song; the woman, who is Maidune, recognizes Nadir and reveals him to the beggars. Tying him, they call the blind Sparamosca so he can avenge himself. Alone with Nadir, and in love, Maidune unties him, and drinks the poison from the phial he carries and which he himself wanted to consume. The king doesn't run; in a final scene each confesses to himself and to the other the change he has gone through: they are older, uglier, sadder, and guiltier. When Sparamosca and the beggars arrive, the king is crying over the dead girl; the blind magician utters the "moral" of the fable: suffering is the measure of being human. "Oh poor King, you have learned how to cry, you too! Now indeed you have arrived."[32]

Although *The Marvelous Island* is a parable of dream-like atmosphere and is expressed in lyrical language, the artist's intellectual interest is the same as in the two first plays and in some later ones: the problem of the inevitability of absurd, "incongruous" suffering and guilt. This is Betti's obsession throughout all his career as a playwright. In fact, in one of his last essays, *Religion and the Theatre*, he repeats, and he underlines the fact that he is repeating, a statement from the Preface to his first play of 1924: the presence of a "bewildering incongruity between our existence and what it ought to be according to the aspirations of our soul."[33] Betti himself indicates awareness of his obsessive interest: "It is probable that what happens to me happens to all playwrights: that is, that I always write basically the same drama. Indeed I will say that I hope it is so."[34]

Keeping in mind this obsession, we would like to touch briefly on two aspects of Bettian criticism. One is the debated point about the social involvement of Betti's characters — whether they exist within a particular economic milieu, whether they feel the impact of historical and social forces,[35] whether they "belong to a country or to a specific time, [and] take their reality directly from being human beings."[36] Although many pages have been written on the subject, the debate is useless if meant to express value judgments. To do this, after Cubism, Surrealism, and *Finnegans Wake*, may be not only useless but unmeaningful.

Another aspect of criticism which we wouldn't take seriously were it not enunciated by some very serious and important critics, is the argument that Betti's psychology is restricted. "It is the psychology of the powerful, even though they [the characters] may later recant or degenerate. The judges of *Landslide* and *Corruption* are the most representative figures of his dramas."[37] This kind of reasoning implies a vision of man completely dependent on socio-economic conditions. It is certainly true that in many of his plays, judges and inquirers of one sort or another are overwhelming presences, but this is only the outer shell of what Betti is really interested in; it is the scaffold with which he was most at home because of his judicial employment, but it is not an artistic or intellectual restriction on the expression of his obsessive interest in existential man.

IV. Un albergo sul porto

In his next play, *Un albergo sul porto* (1930; *An Inn on the Harbor*), Betti completely abandons lyricism and the fable, for a late 18th century Naturalism of vice, brutishness, and violence. Perhaps this sudden reversal shows that Betti has not yet found his own medium for realizing on page and on stage those ghosts in his mind. In regard to this drama the author wrote: "I would like to place certain people and certain feelings naked and alone at the bottom of a long ladder. I would like to see if within themselves, only in themselves, with no help or support, there is, in spite of everything, the capability of climbing up."[38] The author's intentions seem quite clear; in fact he plunges his characters into a kind of no-man's and no-God's land, from whence people are trying to escape and where those who stay permanently, owner and servants of the hotel, or just for a while, sailors or travelling salesmen, appear devoid of any humanity or human dignity; they are all, the strong and the weak, dominated by instinctual forces. The setting is, as the title indicates, a hotel near a port in a Northern country. Poor wretches looking for a better existence have to stop here to pay for and collect documents before they emigrate. The owner, a Greek named Simone, cruelly mistreats and takes advantage of everyone. All hate him and are dominated by him, as if by a diabolical presence. The only pure soul is the young servant, Maria, who is secretly in love with a sailor, Diego, and who dreams of a cleaner life, in spite of the fact that her older sister, one of several girls seduced by Simone, became a prostitute. When Diego sails off, Maria cannot resist Simone, who doesn't tell her of the love message left by Diego at the last moment. When Diego returns, at first he proposes marriage which Maria rejects; later when he discovers her relation to Simone, he, like the others, insults her. Maria, rejected and humiliated, finds in her newly discovered pregnancy the strength to leave: to fight for a dignified life for herself and her baby.

The most relevant characteristic of the style of this play is its unabashed Naturalism. In fact, the play won first prize in 1932 in the National Dramatic Competition, but the committee decided against presenting it because it found in it "so much indecency... so much crudity" and "such naked animality."[39]

It has been observed that in this Naturalism Betti is following Verga's *verismo*: but creativity and a sense of destiny support Verga's pages, and his *verismo* is never an end in itself, while in Betti's play the crudity seems to be used only to render more extraordinary the triumph of motherhood. Maria's redemption at the end is not achieved through moral consciousness but through the instinct of motherhood.[40] Other critics remind us that in Pirandello's *The New Colony* motherhood also redeems.[41]

The play's weakness derives from the author forcing a Naturalistic tone in order to declare his thesis: how people at the bottom of the moral ladder will climb. There is no vibration of a hidden spirituality or feeling of torment beyond instinctual vices, except in one scene when Simone confesses to "being a poor man,"[42] inducing one critic to observe that Simone "in his loneliness, however, thirsting for love and confession, arouses a profound pity."[43] The play makes Diego an unbelievable character: his change toward Maria from saccharine and tender expressions of endearment to sardonic and brutal callousness is gratuitous.[44]

All in all, it is hard to understand, let alone justify, one judgment of the play which characterizes it as "one of the most significant of Betti's works."[45] But there are two elements which give *An Inn on the Harbor* a clear Bettian seal: one is the title itself, characteristically Bettian in its suggestion of enclosure where one is forced to live detached and from where one wishes to flee—other similarly suggestive titles are *The House on the Water*, *The Marvelous Island*, already noted, and later *Night in the House of the Rich Man*, and *Crime on Goat Island*. The other Bettian element is the character, La padrona, who, although listed in the *dramatis personae* doesn't appear; only her voice is twice heard. She dominates the devilish ruler, Simone, who is inexplicably afraid of her. She represents the prototype of that extra-human being who will play an important part in some of Betti's later plays.

Up to now (1930) Betti's theater is a presentation of human beings whose lives are filled with quiet desperation; beings who grasp at existence if not salvation through affirmation of their instincts — *The Mistress of the House* — or through resignation like Francesco in *The House on the Water*; or through an attempted escape or change in their way of life, like Luca in the same play, and Maria in *An Inn on the Harbor*.

In his next three theatrical pieces a change appears in Betti's attitude toward his work. These plays do not remain on one level of suffering; the characters are not contained by their physical and emotional setting, but display a desire for self-knowledge and self-worth, an impulse toward knowledge not emphasized in the first plays. Betti still makes use of symbolical references but now they appear less forced, more organic in the economy of the plot and theme of the work. The main reason for this natural- ness lies in the fact that Betti seems to have removed himself (as an artist) from the immediacy of raw facts and consciously uses them as building blocks to express a personal reaction to reality and to present a complex vision of it. The realism of the earlier plays is either reversed by means of a caricatured and distorted representation — as in the farce *Il diluvio* (*The Flood*) — or defaced by the introduction of extra-human or extraordinary elements — as, especially, in *Landslide*, and somewhat in *Il cac- ciatore d'anitre* (*The Duck Hunter*). In fact, Betti now intro- duces new approaches into his theater: the comedic mode with *The Flood* and which he will make use of later in four other com- edies, albeit not too successfully, and, more important, the con- struction of the play as an inquest or trial, *Landslide* being the most striking of his trial-plays.

V. Landslide

In *Landslide* Betti's ideological and emotional interests come together with the maturing of his artistic experience, as if the play came after a long period of incubation. This can be surmised by the fact that some of the play's details recall some preceding short stories: *Una giornata* ("A Day") for the dripping of the faucet at night which is mentioned by Judge Parsc[46]; *Una bambina sotto un camion* ("A Girl Run over by a Truck") whose plot reminds us of the episode recounted also by the judge — a young girl run over by a bus in which the judge is riding; and *Incidente al 4° km* ("Accident at the Fourth Km") in which a boy commits suicide — one critic[47] considers it the origin of the accident in the play.

The plot unravels as in a detective story; it starts from the crime and goes back into the past to discover the perpetrator. It is the investigation into a landslide which occurred during the excavation for a new railroad line. Parsc, both the investigating and presiding judge, is very sure that "the facts are already clear enough,"[48] and he is convinced the responsible parties can be found in a very short time; in fact he hopes he doesn't have to come back to the Palace of Justice in the afternoon. He wants to agree with Gaucker, the contractor, that the laborers at the site that night are the guilty ones, it is their "negligence and malevolence," or even sabotage[49] which is the cause of the accident. But Goetz, the Prosecutor-general, is not convinced and tells the judge that "the border lines seem to be rather obscure."[50] Judge Parsc is compelled to go further in his investigation. From the laborers responsibility shifts to the contractor, Gaucker, who, saving on expenses, didn't use enough material and men. But towards the end of Act I, Gaucker accuses the Railroad Company in the person of Kurz, its general manager, for forcing upon him an unfair contract; he states that "The responsibility rests ultimately with the Railroad Company."[51] Parsc doesn't want to involve the Company but out of nowhere the Short-sighted Witness starts talking to the judge: "Just keep an eye on the broader issues."[52]

In Act II, the Short-sighted Witness again speaks of "broader issues" and the necessity to "place the thing in perspective."[53] Both Parsc — "I too am unjust," — and Gaucker — "I have been an unprincipled cheat and a scoundrel,"[54] — feel a certain responsibility for the accident. Even Gaucker's wife feels guilty — "Oh God! It was my fault! I should have loved you more."[55] But the Short-sighted Witness continues to accuse the Company in general and Kurz in particular, and insists on looking for a "fixed point."[56] Goetz, the Prosecutor-general, suggests calling as witnesses the dead who were buried under the landslide.

Act III starts with the Short-sighted Witness insisting on the responsibility of Kurz, and with Goetz stating that they "must come to the point. Judgment must be given today." But finally when Kurz appears, he astonishes everybody by revealing the Short-sighted Witness is his only son. Asked by Parsc if he will concede that he is responsible, Kurz ironically states that indeed such a concession would be a relief for everyone, but unfortunately he can't concede it. In fact, although he is not in charge of anything any longer, "nothing has changed.... Wheels turn, trains run on into the night.... The press [that huge mechanism oppressing everybody] is given another twist."[58] To Parsc's insistent questions: "Who is responsible then? Who is responsible?" Kurz accuses everyone including the judge and the audience: "(*He turns to face the audience in the theater*): 'There they are, a lot of small black dots.... As for the old people, it's their children who see to it that they also are crushed...your Honor, you too.... All of you are responsible.'"[59]

Towards the end the three dead men come back to life as witnesses, but even they cannot clear matters. In fact, instead of accusing anyone else, they accuse themselves. Parsc thinks that there is nothing else to do and wants to declare the investigation over, but Goetz insists that he pass judgment. Parsc confesses that he didn't ever and doesn't now believe in what he is doing in his role as a judge. But all want a sentence for all want to be punished for their faults and sins. They want to atone for their individual guilt. Parsc assures them that each one has already been sentenced, since each is suffering. But at this point, the Short-sighted Witness insists that Kurz, the general manager of the Railroad Company, be accused. It seems that all concerned — workers, contractor, the company itself — must share in the responsibility. But if everyone is responsible, no one can be accused. The investigation has proceeded as far as it possibly can. All seem to agree with Kurz that the responsibility lies with the "monstrous machinery" called society.

If this were the main thrust of Betti's play, it would be a superficial work with a predictable ending. However, parallel to the investigation of man as a member of society, the play is also an inquiry into the souls of most of the characters: in fact,

Gaucker, his wife, Judge Parsc himself, and the laborers have already acknowledged their guilt. They have searched into the privacy of their selves and have discovered a lack of purity, of innocence. They can defend their conscious actions before men but they cannot justify themselves before their own eyes. As the play proceeds, one becomes convinced that the more "new facts" are discovered, the less important these facts appear to be. Indeed not only are all concerned responsible, including Parsc and the Short-sighted Witness, but also those who apparently seem not involved at all. This global involvement is emphasized in the penultimate scene of the play by two elements which definitely and finally succeed in jolting our perceptions of it as a play of social responsibility into one of individual destiny.

The first element, formally theatrical, is the accusatory Kurz "turn[ing] to face the audience in the theater" and telling them: "You are responsible!" This is the pivotal moment in the play, for now the audience knows that it is no longer a question of responsibility for the landslide which is at issue but rather of the responsibility for the pain and sorrow of the human condition. This direct involvement of the spectators is not as theatrical as a Pirandellian-like involvement (*e.g.*: If Kurz had mounted the stage from the audience angered by the accusations against him and eager to defend himself, or if a member of the audience had shouted the truth of the family tie between Kurz and the Short-sighted Witness), but it is as effective. In fact, the involvement is not forced or contrived; it appears justified or is at least made acceptable by the fact that the investigation has spread to everyone on stage—except Goetz who is not a "human" *persona*—and from there it seems natural that it should spread to the orchestra. Actually it seems as if the theater has been enlarged and come to encompass not only the orchestra but the entire world.

The second element which jolts our perception of *Landslide* is the reintroduction of The Man Wearing a Shiny Suit. Betti has already prepared the audience; in fact, this character has been seen—jumping into the scene—at the end of Act I protesting his extraneousness not only to the landslide but to the investigation itself. This appearance seemed at the time perplexing and purposeless because illogical and artificial; there was no apparent reason for his intervention. Now with his reappearance his artistic *raison d'être* in the economy of the play is clear. He speaks up during Kurz's last speech when he (Kurz) accuses everyone including the audience. This office worker, this clerk,[60] who is leading a dreary life of misery and hardship, expresses the first defensive reaction which almost every member of the audience instinctively feels. But the clerk — and so the audience — is also involved, if for no other reason than his indifference to his fellow human beings — he doesn't even want to cooperate in the investigation. There is no escaping humanity.

Parallel to the representation of justice in its social and individual aspects, the theme of metaphysical responsibility also threads its way through the play. By focusing on this theme, it emerges that the investigation is baffled by the investigation itself: the more success in uncovering responsibility, the less possible it becomes to indicate responsible individuals. Not only is what is sought not found, but what is found makes absurd the original purpose of the search. In the end, by renouncing justice, the validity of the investigation itself is denied. There is a subtheme which seems to place this senselessness in focus: what some critics[61] call the relation between father and son, referring to Kurz and his son, the Short-sighted Witness. Looked at as a mere contrast between generations, it becomes trivial and uninteresting. In fact, the meaning of this relation is consonant with the import of the entire play: when finally in Act III it is revealed that the Short-sighted Witness has been all along accusing his own father, the audience is edged into a quite complex reaction. For the first two acts the Short-sighted Witness was accusing Kurz, and the audience, if not entirely convinced of the accusation, was certainly agreeing that Kurz should also at least be investigated; when the parental relation is revealed, the audience is not entirely free to react on the sentimental level of being appalled at a son accusing his own father. It has to recoil from this conventional feeling since it has been identifying all along with the Short-sighted Witness. Betti succeeds in shocking his audience out of its emotional conformity. The contrast between father and son is shocking because it is not, and must not be, shocking. Furthermore, in keeping with the overall organization of the play, with its ironic and apparently ambiguous points and counterpoints, this contrast becomes an identification of father and son. In fact, Kurz Senior tells his son: "You are very like me.... You are just like me," and the son answers: "Yes. Just like you."[62] Moreover, even before the father appears, the son shamefully confesses that he used to "mimic"[63] his father. This relentless accuser who seems to be above suspicion, accuses himself just as Judge Parsc does.

The play's most telling subversion of theme, the one that embodies and subsumes the others, is the act of defense which becomes an act of accusation. All the accused—the laborers and Gaucker, the contractor—try to deny their responsibility, to protest their innocence, but by the end of the play they insist on being considered guilty and are ready for, and actually demand, punishment. Yet this desire for punishment is not a longing for justice. In fact, when the victims of the landslide—the three laborers summoned from their death to appear as witnesses— join in the chorus and proclaim, claim even, their own guilt, the play takes a new—and yet not final—turn. It had started as an investigation of the suspects responsible for the physical causes, the actions, which brought about the accident; later it became a psychological inquiry into intention which uncovered gnawing feelings of guilt in both suspects and those who seemed farthest from suspicion—the judge, Gaucker's wife, the audience, society itself—that is, judicial inquiry became a scrutiny of the self. Once it is discovered which actions are the cause of the accident, once it is discovered that everyone's conscience is tainted with guilt, one possible atonement would be death—absolute sacrifice. But when even the dead victims join in the desire for atonement, the judge realizes that the investigation is a buffoonery. "It's all a joke,"[64] and he refuses to conclude with a verdict. At this point the inquiry changes again and for the last time: all want a verdict, not to assign responsibility for the landslide, not to be assured of the purity of their intentions—they all admit to guilt, "We want to be punished"[65]—but to lend reality, substance, to their guilt and their suffering. It isn't any longer a question of justice or innocence but one of meaning, of to be or not to be. It is now an ontological quest, one which will save them from sense-less existence. By receiving a verdict, they are hoping that it will confer purpose upon their lives. Instead of meaninglessness they prefer punishment and pain. There cannot be justice, since justice would imply a division of men into innocent and guilty. Betti in this play—his most· pessimistic and anguished—denies any glimmering of salvation. In a last ironic turn, the verdict is not of condemnation or absolution but of pity. "We declare that these men...need to have something else, higher [than a just sentence]: compassion."[66] There is no verdict, the quest for meaning will always remain a quest.

Some critics believe *Landslide* to be Betti's best play. Indeed, the theatrical assurance and boldness of this work converts the stage into what it becomes when a masterpiece is performed: a magical place. The playwright invents before the audience's eyes a world where the categories and laws of both the real and the probable are audaciously disregarded. Yet *Landslide*'s world is believable. The spectator is easily led into a suspension of disbelief. Although he is not shocked from the beginning into this suspension in the manner of Shakespeare—the appearance of the ghost, let us say, in *Hamlet*—or of Pirandello—the appearance of the "characters" in *Six Characters in Search of an Author*—by the end the spectator has been induced into accepting such similarly impossible phenomena.

In keeping with the reversals of theme and perception, *Landslide* also undergoes a drastic stylistic change. Its beginning is shaped in a realistic style and almost banal manner,[67] but as the play progresses, it slowly sheds more and more of its realistic character and acquires nonrealistic qualities which make aesthetically possible the introduction of phenomena outside the pale of the probable. Betti himself in some sketchy notes drawn before the writing of the play speaks of different phases: the beginning as "objective" or "realistic" and the fourth and last as "metaphysical."[68] In fact, by the end of the first act he has started chipping away, subtly yet substantially, at the realism of the work: a cannon shot announces midday and all the people on the stage suddenly stop speaking and assume puppet-like movements. The import of the cannon shot is not only that it "emphasizes man's subservience to a mechanical routine by bringing everything to a stop,"[69] but that, by generating mechanical, puppet-like

gestures, it also shocks the characters out of their naturalistic behavior during the first act. Their nature is changed. It seems as if
Betti at this point wants to treat his characters as *personae*, in
Pirandellian fashion; his purpose is to prepare the audience for
another kind of play, one different from what they were led to
expect up to now: justice and the discovery of those responsible
for the landslide. What we have here is what Barbetti calls Betti's
"transcendent and dehumanizing tendency."[70]

As the play evolves, Goetz, the Prosecutor-general, also
becomes a character of "magical and super-human nature."[71] His
attitude is too objective, too restrained, too calm to be one of a
Prosecutor-general; in Act II, scene iii, Holand, the court clerk,
says of him: "He is like Olympus."[72] At the end of Act II he
"almost nonchalantly"[73] suggests calling the three dead people as
witnesses.

Another element which leads the play still further into the
fantastic is Kurz's entrance: he appears when he is needed,
without anybody calling him. If, on one hand, his appearance
may symbolize the fact that man doesn't need the prompting of
an outsider to feel the necessity of bringing his guilt to the tribunal of his gnawing and judging conscience, on the other hand,
Kurz's magical entrance finally and completely makes the stage a
stage. The magic of the theater brings him on the stage just as,
some twelve years before, Madame Pace is summoned by the
theater props in *Six Characters in Search of an Author*.

With Kurz on stage, the audience's suspension of disbelief is
total, and it is now prepared for the final challenge of the play:
dead people walking into the scene. Without the audience's preparation there couldn't be a clear theatrical justification for their
presence; moreover, this theatrical justification is the basis for a
more general aesthetic one. The classic Aristotelian justification
argues that what is possible in real life appears improbable ("an
impersuasive possibility") on stage, while what is impossible in
real life appears probable ("a persuasive impossibility") on
stage.[74] That is, there is a quantum leap between the category of
reason and the category of fantasy. Indeed, at the end of the play
the parabola is completed: "from the scanty reality toward the
hallucinating dream atmosphere."[75]

The various theatrical devices prepare us to believe in the dead on an aesthetic level. These devices and the emotional afflatus of the play which spreads a self-consciousness of guilt and a longing for atonement to everyone including the audience lend to the appearance of the dead also a deep psychic justification: live people feel guilty and responsible toward their own ancestors in particular and the dead in general, and they also feel close to the dead in their suffering. *Landslide* is an act or a myth of communion. It is also a statement without hope of man's predicament, but as Betti once observed: "All I can do is clumsily try to prove certain things again...starting from zero.... One must not be afraid of [the] desert."[76] So Camus's *The Myth of Sisyphus*, is meant "as a lucid invitation to live and create, in the very midst of the desert."[77]

But the question remains: What to prove by starting from zero?—The various changes, reversals, turning points in *Landslide* are new starts. Paul Klee states that the artist has an "essential image of creation..., as Genesis, rather than...the image of nature, [as a] final product. Then he permits himself the thought that the process of creation can today hardly be complete, and he sees the act of world creation stretching from the past to the future. Genesis eternal!"[78] As for Betti, every moment is a zero moment between chaos and apocalypse.

VI. Il cacciatore d'anitre

Il cacciatore d'anitre (1934; *The Duck Hunter*), written two years after *Landslide*, is also an instance of Betti's development from realism toward a more symbolic and abstract form of theater. In a town near the Atlantic Ocean—the stage directions suggested Norway to Orazio Costa, director of the *Accademia* in Rome, the company that produced the first belated performance of the play in 1940—Michial, a very old man who is about to die, owns everything of value. He lives with a niece, Fausta; two more distant relatives, Aurelio and Marco, friends since childhood, live nearby. One of them is destined to inherit the immense fortune, but while Aurelio obeys and flatters the old man, Marco continues to be, as he has always been, scornful, proud, and pure—always wishing that the Regent—an otherwordly all-powerful being—will come to bring justice to the town. Yet Marco cannot resist the temptation set by Ignazio, Michial's secretary, who implants in him a lust for wealth on one hand and a suspicion of Aurelio on the other; Marco even repudiates Elena, the woman he loves, and their child, so he can be free to become engaged to Fausta, the surest way to acquire the inheritance.

Elena runs away. Marco, repentant, runs after her to ask her forgiveness, but she has already thrown herself and their child from a cliff. Michial derides Marco for his former pride and conceit in considering himself above everyone else in town; he felt ashamed because of him, but now that Marco has lost the last remnant of his dignity, the old man feels "a great satisfaction,... in showing God what a worm [Marco is]...."[79] Then Michial himself falls off the cliff. Marco is suspected of having pushed him and is arrested. In order to save himself, Marco demonstrates his innocence, but it is not enough, and he surrenders completely to corruption by agreeing to bribe the judge. Free at last, powerful, and unholy, he still longs for purity when he faces Aurelio. But Ignazio, the tempting demon, stabs Marco to death rather than lose him to goodness. After his death the Regent appears.

In *Landslide* Betti uses all the characters to produce a choral impression since he is primarily interested in presenting the human condition; in *The Duck Hunter* he focuses his attention on one character, and he depicts his agon after having sinned. In fact, except for Marco, all the *personae* are figures without any real psychological depth; their only purpose is to provide the setting in which the protagonist acts out his destiny. He is alone both on a social and psychological level—he is unable to communicate with and convince the people surrounding him of his intentions—and on an artistic level—he is the only person seen in the round. The author's intent is to represent human destiny emblematically through Marco's parable, but the play falters at times into an "abstract"[80] tone.

Betti wants to represent the fall of man, the loss of Eden: Marco symbolizes post-lapsarian man who after the fall not only is unable to regain his state of grace but moves farther and farther from his original purity. Nevertheless, when we meet Marco at the beginning, he seems already to have committed his original sin. He appears much too proud to be a hero, pure and guiltless. In his first moments on stage Marco states: "I prize my dog's sneezes much more than the...opinions of this pleasant little town."[81] Michial sarcastically calls him a "noble lion, a haughty angel."[82] In the next scene he again calls him "a haughty angel,"[83] one of the "White eagles, archangels in exile,"[84] a "proud eagle,"[85] a "white dolphin," and a "lion."[86] One of the minor characters calls him "Mr. Great Man."[87]

These epithets can easily be explained as the expression of the envy a superior man provokes, but Marco's pride, since the beginning, is such that it seems to deny him any goodness. One must deal with the question and decide it: Is Marco, at the beginning of the play, pure? If Marco is, then it is possible to interpret the play as a tragedy "of the corrupting power of riches,"[88] or as purity succumbing to the temptations of the worldly, or as "the struggle between the spiritual values and the power of riches."[89] If it is assumed that at the beginning Marco is innocent, then not only must we think with Leonida Repaci that he "lacks...interior coherence"[90] but that the entire play is incoherent. Marco in fact would be a cartoon character; for the suddenness of his change from innocence to corruption, even to cruelty—he abandons his beloved Elena and their child—is unjustifiable; his character would not be "psychologically acceptable."[91] For Marco to be coherent and for the play to be meaningful, he should have capitulated to the forces of evil only towards the end. His surrender seems to take place in Act III, scene v, when the judge, the High Auditor, in asking for a bribe, tempts him "to sell paradise."[92] And when Marco does, the court clerk declares: "You sold your soul to the devil."[93] But such a play would be different from the one Betti wrote. It is not at this point that Marco loses his innocence. The last request of the High Auditor is: "be frank with yourself, and choose."[94] And his last statement, after Marco agrees to give a bribe in order to win the case, is: "I understood it right away, as soon as you entered the room, that deep down in you there was this. Yes, you had already decided since the beginning. I think you'll win."[95] In other words,

Marco doesn't take here the pivotal step from virtue to vice, from purity to sin; rather he completes the process of losing his innocence which he started long ago.

This seems, of course, obvious, but what is not so obvious is that Betti presents the audience with a fallen hero at the outset. When Marco enters, he has already sinned; he has already lost Eden. His is the original sin of pride. In fact, at the beginning he feels superior to the people around him. We have quoted his utterance about his dog. A little later, he states — hyperbolically but revealingly — that he would prefer to die than blush in front of anybody.[96] He even thinks that as a child he "had in himself a small spark of God's fire."[97] He "made fun of the rich."[98] He didn't want to stay in that wretched town "where he was born."[99] Later on, we learn also that Marco used to seduce the "nicer fishermen's daughters."[100]

That Betti didn't create a play about the corruption of an innocent is also evidenced by the fact that the play doesn't end with Marco's final corruption. There is another long scene which takes place days later, in which Marco confronts death; immediately after, the Regent, the first of several eschatological figures in Betti's theater, to whom Marco had written when he was a little boy and whose advent he has always wished, finally appears. The play ends with the dead protagonist facing the extra-human figure he was unable to face while alive.

So Marco has never been innocent. Instead of depicting the corruption of an innocent man, the play is about a man, burdened by his corrupt humanity, who tries to discover values and actions that will allow him to realize, in Marco's words, that "there must be something which makes it worthwhile being in this world."[101] Marco, though not innocent, is a modern hero, and his tragedy is a modern tragedy. It is not by chance that Betti only once subtitles one of his plays *Modern Tragedy*. Marco is a tragic hero because he doesn't have a choice, he cannot avoid his destiny; he is a modern hero because he is gnawed by the worm of self-consciousness; at times, he doubts his intentions. In fact, many of his statements reveal him trapped in his limited humanity: "What I wanted was something else."[102] "I didn't want to remain in this wretched town."[103] "I don't want to waste in petty envies, useless acts, stupid satisfactions, the mysterious spark of my life."[104] "I am not a being destined to crawl in the dust and eat it."[105] And he has always wished for the Regent to set things straight and perhaps give order and meaning to existence. In fact, toward the end Betti, through Ignazio, contrasts the Regent with chaos: "The Regent will never hear your voice."[106] And later on the same page, Ignazio states that the injustice in the world must lead one "to believe that there is nothing above us, nothing but chaos."[107]

Marco is not only aspiring in vain for what it is impossible to achieve, but he is also aware of his human condition as a fallen man. After lowering himself to flattery and envy, he exclaims: "What have I done, then? In such a short time, I forswore my opinions, my youth, and all that was dear to me."[108] Later on, in the same scene, he reflects: "And perhaps really there was, hidden in me, a desire for those things that make life a little bit happier."[109] After Michial falls from the cliff, Marco admits to himself that he thought of pushing the old man and so is guilty; later he is convinced that he is a worm and that the people accusing him may be right.

In spite of his aspirations and his awareness, he succumbs to pettiness, greed, cruelty, and hate. We see him deluding himself about the inheritance, claiming that with it "there would be beautiful things to do,"[110] or claiming he can bring a new sense of justice to "the town, and also work, happiness, friendship, peace."[111] His "purpose is to do something good, strong, useful."[112]

Even after the favorable judgment he thinks that his "life was wasted."[113] His last words, before he dies, are: "Perhaps, in all of this, there was a mistake."[114] He dies just before the Regent arrives; he is denied the opportunity of self-accusation, and, with this denial, he is also denied the certainty of whether or not his life was a mistake; he is even denied pity. He started impure and hopeful, he ends impure and hopeless. We underline the denial of pity in order to contrast the ending of this play with the end of *Landslide*. The two plays focus on different interests: *Landslide* presents a guilt-ridden human chorus which wants to be cleansed of its guilt by seeking that purgatorial punishment which will permit an ultimately liberating absolution; *The Duck Hunter* stages humanity not as a chorus but in the protagonist Marco who also strives in vain to raise himself from the ignoble weaknesses of his nature. Both plays represent dark moments in Betti's perception of the human condition. But it seems that with the end of *The Duck Hunter* Betti wants to convey a pessimism more searing than in *Landslide*. In the earlier play there hangs over the chorality of the characters an undying, albeit negative, brotherhood of commiseration: at the end the judge, instead of condemning, treats error and sin with pity. In *The Duck Hunter* there is no mellowing of any kind: the hope in an extra-human being remains a mere hope. The Regent, in fact, will arrive only after Marco's death. If there is a meaning, if one's actions and intentions are pure, it can be known only from the perspective of an afterlife. The humanity of *Landslide* is seen *sub specie temporis*, of *The Duck Hunter*, *sub specie aeternitatis*. The glimpse of an afterlife hardly lends the play "a happy conclusion,"[115] as one critic says; we don't believe the play ends optimistically.

Perhaps because it is the first time that Betti introduces into his theater an eschatological dimension, this play appears theatrically weak. It is "static and literary."[116] In *Landslide* there are visual, *theatrical* techniques which ease the spectator into a suspension of his disbelief; in *The Duck Hunter*, the protagonist is developed too scantily and his conversion and reconversion, toward riches and Elena, are too quick to move the audience toward a noble and tragic pathos.

The most "literary" element in the play is the character of Ignazio, the tempter; he represents Marco's dark side, but he is not theatrically believable and he remains only a symbol. The fact that he is in love with Fausta is said but not sufficiently staged. Yet the play is an important one for the playwright, for a great number of his later plays will advance, in a more theatrically successful manner, the eschatological dimension. This play is also important in the author's intellectual and emotional life. In the next four years, until 1938, Betti will write only four light and superficial comedies with middle-class *milieux*, his only attempts at laughter. Did he attempt an escape from his "heroic pessimism?"[117]

Chapter 3

Retreat Toward Laughter
(1934–1938)

*We shall not allow ourselves to be misled by the contrast
between the comic and the sublime into forgetting that they
serve a common purpose: the mastery of an inner danger*
(*Ernst Kris*, Psychoanalytic Explorations in Art).

I. Il diluvio

Although *Il diluvio* (*The Flood*) was written in 1931, before
both *Landslide* and *The Duck Hunter*, we will consider it at this
point so that we may deal with all of Betti's comedies in one
place. *The Flood* (first performed in 1942) is Betti's first comic
play, and also his most serious comedy. It also represents his first
withdrawal from the realistic mode of his first theatrical production, and perhaps the play's novelty seems more important in
the intellectual career of the playwright than the play itself. As we
have already noted, the caricatured and the grotesque represent a
kind of detachment from realism. They denote in Betti's development a shift toward a somewhat more abstract and symbolic
method of constructing his plays.

The title of this farce — the author's subtitle is *Farce in Three
Acts* — points to a new apocalyptic flood to wash the world of its

31

ugliness and evil. Specifically, the title refers to a play which the protagonist Arcibaldo Mattia, professor of bookkeeping, is writing. As in farce, the events on stage are absurd, unbelievable, laughable, and unreal. It takes place in a petty-bourgeois household were Arcibaldo lives with his very young and too attractive wife, Clelia, a domineering mother-in-law, and the undisciplined little rascal of a teen-age brother-in-law. This arrangement is reason enough for farce but what gives Arcibaldo no respite is lack of money. He doesn't have enough for a bearable, let alone respectful and dignified, way of living. A constant and painful reminder of his financial hardship are his creditors: the landlord, the pharmacist, the grocer, the innkeeper, and as he tells us, "the pork-butcher who mistreats you, mortifies you, despises you out loud, because your purchases are limited and reasonable."[1]

In the first scene Leonia, the mother-in-law's sister enters with her daughter, Fatma, and asks Arcibaldo to please pretend to be their respective husband and father, the real one having left them long ago. A millionaire, Lindoro Polten-Bemoll, whom they met the past summer and who showed interest in Fatma, is coming to visit them, and it seems more dignified if they are not alone. Arcibaldo, already beside himself, should also lend his house, theirs being in a poor neighborhood. He is ready to refuse with scorn to participate in such a scheme, but he capitulates when Leonia flatters him as an author, and lets him glimpse the possibility of being launched by Bemoll. As soon as the creditors suppose that Arcibaldo may have such a rich relative, they come to offer anything needed to set the "hook" for Bemoll: furniture, carpets, linen, china. The innkeeper even offers *to lend* a dinner on conditions that nobody touch it, except for the millionaire — the dinner is for the celebration of a christening. He will also send the cartoon chickens used for display purposes in this window.

Bemoll is pseudosophisticated, decadent, interested mainly in the pleasure of his senses; he exploits everyone around him without difficulty since people are happy to be exploited in the belief that contact with a millionaire will elevate them to a higher level of sensibility and social status. He is the most accomplished character in the farce. Betti succeeds in creating a puppet-like character. Bemoll's trick, used several times, of having his secretary finish his sentences is most felicitous; so is his trick of having his secretary hit him on the head with a brush to remind him of the time. Some traits of Bemoll's physique suggest to Di Pietro[2] a caricature of D'Annunzio.

Act II starts with the dinner. This scene and the fifth of Act I, during which the landlord, the pharmacist, and the grocer bring to the dining room the best they can find in their own homes in order to impress the millionaire, are the only scenes of pure farce in the play. The movements are clownish and remind Cologni of "the first comical sequences of the American film."[3]

During dinner Arcibaldo cannot stop people from eating the borrowed food, from breaking an expensive borrowed glass, or from dirtying the rare borrowed carpet; he also starts eating, invoking "the trumpets of the Apocalypse,"[4] and declares that everybody nourishes a corpse, that "man swims in a whirl-pool...of his own excrements."[5] He is mocked by everyone, including Bemoll, who meanwhile seduces a most willing Clelia, Arcibaldo's wife, instead of her cousin. At the end of the dinner, thinking that the woman he is after is Fatma, Arcibaldo helps the creditors lock his wife and Bemoll in his bedroom. The creditors are aware of who is in the room and believe that Arcibaldo also knows. They are in awe of his courage in allowing himself to be so coolly cuckolded. When Leonia, bitter because it is not her daughter who is about to be seduced, screams the truth at him, Arcibaldo becomes demonstrative; even now the creditors think he is playing a part and second him in what they think is a pretense; but when he wants to open the door, they stop him. They guard the door as if it were their self-interest.

At the beginning of Act III Arcibaldo, still hoping that nothing has happened, is ready to forgive Clelia, but when Clelia enters, she accuses him of being ugly, cowardly, smelly, and old; she reveals her disgust for him and her readiness to leave him. At the end of the scene she pushes his manuscript of *The Flood* off the table; it separates on the floor, as she utters her last words: "You can keep *The Flood*!"[6] The creditors arrive. Convinced that Arcibaldo is now under Bemoll's protection, they give him money and admire his beauty, sensibility, intelligence, and *The Flood*. When Bemoll arrives, Arcibaldo accuses him of being a worm, a disgusting being, and after slapping and kicking him, is ready to exit with his "nitroglycerine," *The Flood*. But his young brother-in-law has given it to the garbage collector. Arcibaldo takes a gun, shoots toward the ceiling, falls on the floor, and dies of heart failure.

The end is not tragicomic as some critics[7] believe, nor tragic; at most, it may arouse pity; in fact it is unheroic[8] since Arcibaldo doesn't shoot himself; neither is it comic since comedy per se denies death. Comedy may accommodate mocking impotence or old age, beating or cuckoldry but not death, or at least not the death of a major character. The play is not a pure farce, as the author believed it to be. He had stated: "My first idea was to write a tragedy.... I realized that instead of a tragedy I wrote a farce."[9] Whether one takes these words at face value, as several critics do, or as an afterthought on the author's part, when he was judging the play, doesn't matter. In both cases the statement suggests why at some performances it was received with catcalls, shouts, and whistling. In the play there are scenes full of vitality and zest, of buffoonery, which clearly show Betti's theatrical ability and ease in using dialogue and movement in order to create an atmosphere on the stage. This comedic aspect reminds some critics of the comedies of Machiavelli, Bruno, Bibbiena,[10] *Le cocu magnifique* (*The Magnificent Cuckold*) by Crommelynck, *L'uomo, la bestia e la virtù* (*Man, Beast, and Virtue*) by Pirandello, and also Feydeau.[11] To Di Pietro,[12] among others, it recalls *La maschera e il volto* (*Mask and Face*) by Chiarelli, especially after Arcibaldo finds out he is a cuckold.

But the lightness of these comic scenes is weighted down by the fact that they are among quite ponderous ones. Seriousness, even solemnity at times in this play, and laughter don't coalesce into a unified vision. Elements of the tragic, whether intentional or not, do exist here. There is also the problem of social satire: is it the central element of the play, a revelation of "the savagery of [Betti's] attack on conventional bourgeois morality?"[13] Or, is the central element an interest in "ultimate things" and the central conflict between time and eternity, life and death, man and the great mystery"?[14] Another critic is of the opinion that "If...the farce posits...a general problem [without] precise determination of space and time, [and it] insists on 'principles' universally valid for every man, the allusions...[to] the Italian bourgeoisie of the thirties are [nevertheless] evident."[15] These discrepancies don't derive from the fact that the critics have different personal views of the farce but that they focus their attention on different aspects of a theatrical work which doesn't possess a focus at all. Betti himself realized this lack of unity when he observed that his intention was to write a tragedy but that he had written a farce. So, if some parts appear successful when viewed as elements in a farce, they lose their impact when considered in the entire economy of the play.

This incongruence is especially evident when Arcibaldo acts farcically. For example,[16] when Giacinto, the teen-age brother-in-law, wets him with his water pistol, Arcibaldo, drying his face, exclaims: "Is it water, at least? Is it water?"[17] As one critic says: "It is a kind of humor demanded by the genre,"[18] meaning, of course, by farce. Another farcical moment is in scene v of Act III when Arcibaldo is frightened on seeing the rope he took out for hanging jump by itself; he tries to catch it until he realizes it is another of Giacinto's jokes. In fact, the same trick had been used by Feydeau.[19] However, these remain isolated notes, Betti wants to use Arcibaldo to censure society's mores; in this character he becomes quite serious as a judge of the others. But the humor of the two laugh-provoking *genre* scenes is too lowbrow, to undignified, too brainless, *i.e.*, too farcical, for Arcibaldo to be taken seriously in other parts of the play. Only if he had hanged himself would the rope scene have made sense as black humor.

The play is a pure and simple farce in respect of those characters unencumbered by the author's serious intention: the creditors, especially the innkeeper, are unforgettable caricatures; and the women utter one-liners worthy of the best comediennes. When the mother-in-law says: "For such a man I would close one eye," Clelia answers: "So would I," Leonia adds "I would close two," and Arcibaldo, "I would close three."[20] Perhaps the most burlesque one-liner is pronounced by Leonia in describing Bemoll: "What intelligence! What finesse! What socks!"[21]

Yet if, on one hand, Arcibaldo is too undignified to be convincing in the role of censor, on the other, he is too complex merely as a clown. Indeed, Betti deals with ultimate questions in this play, but not in the sense some critics have meant; in the main character the author embodies the existential paradox; Arcibaldo appears as a Kierkegaardian "synthesis of the soulish and bodily"[22]; he experiences "the condition of individuality with finitude."[23] Arcibaldo's symbolic self reveals itself in his desire to reform society; his aspiration is to spiritualize the creaturality which attaches to his bodily functions. In fact, in moments of weakness he reveals a gluttonous appetite. In Act I, scene i, he remarks: "I don't have great desires, deep down. I would like to eat fried apples with sugar."[24] He again mentions his desire for fried apples in Act II, scene iv,[25] and in Act II, scene v, the innkeeper tries to comfort him by telling him he will be able to eat them every day.[26] His reaction to water squirting is another expression of creaturality: "Is it real water, at least?"[27] When Arcibaldo, exalted by the wine and his own rhetoric, shouts during the dinner that he is going to blow up a society based on false ideals, we learn that the nitroglycerine in his play *The Flood* is really human excrement which will flood the world. In the words of Ernest Becker: "When men really want to protest against artificialities, when they rebel against the symbolisms of culture, they fall back to basic chemistry."[28]

Betti doesn't develop this human paradox—he only touches it lightly—but it is this aspect of the play that doubtless convinces some critics, Fabbri among them, that *The Flood* is "among the most beautiful things of our Italian theater."[29] We would agree, however, with Nicola Chiaramonte who thinks the plot offers three possibilities: "pure and simple farce, satirical, or ferocious and dark farce, [and that Betti] had not chosen any [but] persisted in working at random."[30] The play has never been successfully performed and was greeted with "whistles and insults"[31] when the De Filippos staged its première on 28 January 1943.

From 1934, when *The Duck Hunter* was written, to 1938, the year of *Notte in casa del ricco* (*Night in the Rich Man's House*), Betti composed four light comedies which represent a departure from the more ponderous obsessions and interests of his career.

Almost all[32] the critics agree these are minor works, and they feel
the need to discover a specific motivation behind them, a motivation clearly different from that of the "tragic" plays. No one
would dream of asking the same question in regard to Shakespeare or Pirandello, since with them, their talent and their
success in comedy is justification enough. One would be hard put
to notice such a talent in Betti—hence the need to justify him
through extra-artistic or personal considerations. Betti himself
gives an autobiographical reason: "He wrote them out of wicked-
ness.... One day a bourgeois author told him in a condescending
tone, as if speaking to a pupil: 'Why don't you try to get close to
the public?' A little bit upset, he wrote these comedies to demon-
strate that it wasn't hard to be applauded."[33] This may be true,
but it is not the entire truth. In fact, as G.H. McWilliam observes, "The objection to this explanation is that one play would
have been adequate. Why did he feel it necessary to write four?"[34]

But one can look for a more intimate explanation. Di Pietro,
for instance, states that these works, "exactly because they lack
vis dramatica, are coherent and valid witnesses of a trustful,
serene state of mind."[35] This argument agrees with the critic's
interpretation of Betti's preceding drama, *The Duck Hunter*; he
perceives, at the end of the play, in the appearance of an otherworldly figure, a "happy conclusion."[36] Di Pietro also notes, as
proof of Betti's serenity, some changes the playwright made in his
preceding work; they are, according to Di Pietro, "documents" of
Betti's more "optimistic" beliefs. For example, the changed end
of *The House on the Water*: in the first version Elli, the heroine,
drowns, in the later one, she lives.

We cannot, however, accept Di Pietro's explanation. The
appearance of the Regent hardly mitigates the pessimism of *The
Duck Hunter*, and if Betti changed the end of *The House on the
Water*, eight years after, in an apparently optimistic way, one
could infer that the author was deeply disturbed by the original
ending and that this disturbance is a sign of inner struggle not of
serenity. Betti wrote the comedies, we would like to suggest, for a
reason opposite Di Pietro's. He may have found the pessimism in
the two plays which precede the comedies unbearable. His religiosity prevented him from accepting a world devoid of the

immanent ideal, a life that can be justified only in terms of the afterlife; it is the old problem that every religious person must encounter and solve—how to accept evil in a world created by an omniscient God. Betti tried to escape a direct confrontation with his obsessions through his writings; he needed time to recoup his forces. For "the comic and the sublime...serve a common purpose: the mastery of an inner danger,"[37] and "the comic effects a reduction of mental energy [while] the sublime calls for a surplus expenditure of this,"[38] Betti's state of mind was such that he could accept the superficial challenge of an older colleague; Mc-William's objection, that one comedy would have been enough, doesn't hold.

That this phase is an escape seems to be confirmed by Betti himself when, seven years after the composition of his first comedy, he wrote: "It is my opinion that the main stream of my theater...doesn't pass through there [the comedies]."[39] The titles themselves imply escape: one deals with "a beautiful Sunday," one with holidays, a third with dreams or daydreaming, and the last with a fable. Whatever the motivations, conscious or unconscious, behind them, the author himself considered them escapist. It was a period of his life when he preferred not to face his darker self; he preferred to face society which he found much easier. If tragedy is the struggle with oneself and comedy the one between the individual and society, Betti's *oeuvre* seems to fit these definitions. The characters of his four comedies deal with one of the most persistent of social institutions, marriage.

II. Una bella domenica di settembre

Una bella domenica di settembre (*A Beautiful September Sunday*) was written in 1936 and premièred in 1937, without success. Act I takes place in front of the office of the prefecture, where Federico Norburi, district councilman, is supposed to chair a very important meeting. Carlo Lusta, an "adjunct temporary vice-subarchivist,"[40] arrives late and without the key to his office where the report he had so carefully prepared is kept. Since it is Sunday, Carlo's landlady didn't wake him up on time; he had left the key handy, not in the usual but in a special place, and then forgot where. So he waits outside begging the janitor to go and see if by chance the key is in the door-lock.

Meanwhile Norburi's wife, Adriana, their children, Roberto and Lia, and Lia's boyfriend, Miche, arrive in front of the building to wait for Norburi; today they will celebrate Adriana's birthday with a picnic on the shore of the lake. But the young people get tired of waiting and leave. Adriana sits on a bench for a while, and when she decides to leave, she forgets her purse. Carlo sits on the same bench and picks it up. A nearby policeman thinks he is a suspicious character, but when Adriana comes back, she pretends to know him. They sit together and talk. Their sadness — she is lonely, he is sure of having lost his job — brings them to a certain desire to confide in each other; yet they are not entirely sincere because they would still like to hide the truth from their own selves. Carlo tells of how he quit his boring job in the office and how he travelled all over the world including China — in fact he has been to…Tokyo. Adriana tells of how lonely a friend of hers feels; of how this beautiful September Sunday will pass and she herself will not have gone to enjoy the lake; of how, when old, she will regret it together with so many other things. Adriana has forgotten her house key (another misplaced key!), and she accepts Carlo's invitation to go to the Nymphs' Shore, a noisy, cheap, and somewhat equivocal café, where those smiling red-faced servant girls, envied by Adriana for their happy thoughtlessness, go every Sunday to meet and dance with their boyfriends.

Act II takes place in the café: while they drink some wine Adriana speaks of her husband's loving attention, but soon she takes off her thin mask and tells the truth. She reveals her longing for love, and her desire to be treated with more consideration by her husband and her children: she confesses her fear of growing old, and her desire for a different life. Carlo dreams out loud that indeed "one could be…who knows what, a hero, why not?"[41] Meanwhile the café is filled with screams and laughter, and in the adjacent garden some young people are having fun, Lia among them. The police, Norburi, and Roberto arrive, but Adriana has already been able to take her daughter away.

In Act III, Adriana arranges an engagement between Lia and her boyfriend. She tries to excuse Lia's behavior by telling her husband and son that she herself had gone to the café, but they cannot understand her meaning: they believe that she means she went there to protect her daughter. Adriana realizes that she is an angel for them, "but a wooden angel."[42] When Lia's father and brother see that the "scandal" is over, each goes his own way, Norburi to an appointment very important for his career, and Roberto to his university friends. Adriana dismisses her would-be seducer Carlo with a maternal kiss, and remains, once again, alone, accepting, with hardly a "whimper," her domesticity, her old age, and the new role she envisions as a grandmother.

The co-protagonists, Adriana and Carlo, both represent and express the desire for disengaging themselves from bourgeois pettiness. The comedy of such an assumption should derive from the superficiality and cautiousness of their attempt to shed the conventions of society. The plot is quite funny: an escape to a café where some of the patrons engage in the risqué behavior of squirting seltzer water. There is laughter in the timidity of the co-protagonists, who assume their gestures and language are desecrative, not just weak and superficial. Adriana and Carlo are so ingrained in their way of seeing the world, their ideas and ideals are so set in an accepted mold of propriety that whatever they may believe they are doing, in reality they just confirm their uncritical subservience to received mores in displays of pettiness.

Adriana accepts the invitation to go to the café, only because she is locked out of her home. They will go to a café where there are rooms reserved for lovers only after a pompous and solemn promise by Carlo that he will be a perfect gentleman. Adriana's greatest thrill will be the chance of pulling the handle of the café's pinball machine. That this act could represent a sexual displacement and that it should be pregnant with subconscious meaning (castration, self-castration?) is not only far from Adriana's consciousness but also from the author's ultimate interest. Some critics have mentioned Feydeau when talking of Betti's comedies, but the recollection is not valid. It is enough to imagine this pinball machine scene as Feydeau would have presented it, full of double entendres, of coquettish gestures and words. The humor in Betti rests on the fact that Adriana pulled the knob too hard and broke it and that Carlo is worried about the fifty cents it costs; it is an adolescent laughter without depth. Not that Betti is prudish, for in later plays he will deal with sex in an open and almost crude manner (in *Irene innocente* and *The Inquiry*); and he will write about incest (in *Acque turbate* [*Troubled Waters*]). What prevents Betti from taking advantage of the situation in this comedy is his unwillingness to make fun of his protagonists. He appears too concerned with preserving the *status quo* of the institution of marriage. Such earnestness excludes any "serious" *vis comica*. In fact, the author tips the scale so much that he is unable to hold or even arouse the audience's interest: from the beginning when Adriana remains alone and lonely, the stage is set either for tragedy, pathos, bathos, or comedy depending on her depth of self-consciousness and sensitivity. But Betti chooses not to develop any of these moods.

Carlo's situation is also one that could extend from tragedy to farce. One possibility is for a young man, desperate to the point of suicide, to meet an older and pleasant woman; and from their short encounter, this young man would recover sufficient energy and desire to go on living. This is the plot and theme of Stefan Zweig's short story, "Twenty-four Hours in a Woman's Life," but it is not Betti's intention, and the fact that he rejects a serious development per se is not an error. Actually, it is to the author's credit, to construct a comedy from an "open" situation—and, as it has been noticed the plot is indeed comical. Carlo, a comical figure, is a schlemiel: in what could be the most important day of his career, everything goes wrong. He may lose his job and his "rank." If Carlo had found a similar partner in Adriana, a light and delightful piece could have ensued, but she is not a comic character. The author has refused to contaminate her "purity"; for the entire play she remains on the pedestal of her wifehood and motherhood; she even becomes lyrical, with great sensibility, and, as one critic says, "spiritual superiority."[43]

When the two protagonists come together, Carlo, who at first is genuinely comic, later utters thoughts so ponderous that he becomes ridiculous. The audience is denied the laughter aroused by a giddy woman. She dismisses him with a maternal kiss.

The last scene recapitulates in a nutshell all the inadequacies and ambiguities of the play: Adriana remains alone on the stage and whispers *with real anguish*: "Grandmother." Then she repeats it with a *certain sweetness*. The third and last time she utters it *with a smile*. It appears that the character, whom Betti had placed above all the others, endowing her with gentility and sensibility, is forced into a stupor-like smile in expectation of her new status. But the change is forced upon the character, for the passage from *real anguish* to the *smile* is too swift. When she whispers "Grandmother" with *real anguish*, Adriana appears as one of those Pirandellian characters trapped forever in the hell of the unavoidable routine of everyday existence. So, at the end, she is denied her moment of self-knowledge. In the same way she has never been given a chance of escaping: Carlo is not a serious tempter, not even a second-rate seducer, let alone an Iago or a Mephistopheles. But the author's thesis in this comedy is—as he wrote in an unpublished note—to present "the solidity and beauty of the family which becomes evident as soon as the most futile misunderstanding seems to place them in danger."[44] If for a moment the spectator is reminded of a Chekhovian melancholy, the last expectant smile—lowering the tone of the anguish—distances the end from the Russian playwright's characteristic mood of desperate resignation. Chekhov, we may imagine, would have reversed the three final stage directions: *with a smile, with a certain sweetness, with real anguish.*

III. Summertime

Il paese delle vacanze (1937) is the only one of Betti's comedies translated into English (as *Summertime* by Henry Reed in 1955). As the subtitle, *Idyll in Three Acts*, suggests, the author is interested only in staging a love story. Of course without marriage lurking in the background the idyll would not exist. There is "no serious attempt to equip the play with a serious 'message'."[45] Its "total lack of commitment"[46] appears amazing, when compared to the rest of Betti's *oeuvre*, including the comedies. In fact, Betti works within a genre tradition: all the characters are the "conventional figures"[47] belonging to the "rose" theater, and they are "stylized."[48] Far from being a mistake, this tactic is appropriate for such a feather-light work; and Betti's subtitle indicates that he is, in the words of G.H. McWilliam, "aware of the limitations of this type of play."[49]

With the Foreword (only *The Mistress of the House* has a Preface; there is also a technical Foreword to *Husband and Wife*) Betti underscores his detached attitude to the piece and almost "warns" the audience, through the director and the actors, to judge the two main characters appropriately. He writes: "Francesca is a calm and sweet young lady like many others: her clear vocation is to get married and have children. Alberto is an agreeable young man like many others: his singularity consists in not being singular."[50] "Like many others" tells us in advance not to expect any psychological penetrations. The stage will be populated by stock characters in a playful plot, far from the harsh realities of living or life. In fact, this is Betti's most successfully escapist work and the most successful of them at the box office. At its first performance, in 1942, "The public applauded five times after the first act; at the end of the second act there was a momentary dissent, followed by five curtain calls; and two curtain calls at the end of the third act. The author appeared with the actors after the second and third acts."[51]

The plot is very tenuous. Act I, the most lively and fastpaced, takes place in the garden of Francesca's aunt, Cleofe, which is adjacent to the garden of Alberto's aunt, Ofelia. Francesca is in love with Alberto, and she had been trying to make him notice it. But he seems quite uninterested—they have known one another since childhood. Today, they will go to the yearly picnic in the mountains nearby, and Francesca, determined to reveal her love, will ask him to marry her. But Alberto announces he is not going. He is leaving instead for the city, for a new and important job in a bank. Then two telegrams arrive informing him of the arrival of Noemi and her brother, Consalvo, who wants to force Alberto to marry her, thereby repairing the scandal the inexperienced Alberto quite innocently precipitated. Alberto, afraid to face the irate Consalvo, decides to go on the picnic.

In Act II, in the mountains, Francesca speaks of marriage to

Alberto, and he is convinced that it indeed seems the best solution. But Alberto has misunderstood, he thinks Francesca is
trying to convince him to marry Noemi. In a rage she pushes him
off a cliff, a very thorny but very shallow cliff, and runs away. In
the last act, Alberto comes to the home of a farmer in search of
Francesca, and so do Noemi and Consalvo. In order to defend
Alberto from their trap, Francesca insinuates that she has been
seduced by him. All ends well with the two protagonists reconciled and happy. But Francesca, in spite of her name, doesn't
radiate the eternal feminine. No matter how successful the idyll
may have been, we cannot help thinking that this comedy will
have difficulty in finding a sophisticated public.

IV. I nostri sogni

I nostri sogni (1937; *Our Dreams*) was a success at its first
performance in Parma, on November 7, 1937, and was a triumph
in Milan in 1941.[52] The general theme is the same as in *A Beautiful September Sunday*: the desire to change one's circumstances.
The dream of Titi, the protagonist, and of her parents, is to
achieve the social and economic status, with the elegance and refinement they think it brings, of the middle class. Both Titi and
Adriana long for a life of gentility and love which they cannot
experience in their own home.

In town a new branch of Toons and Son Co. is opening, and
in their new offices, not yet furnished, the penniless Leo, always
followed by his friend Louis, introduces himself to the company
director, Posci, who has just been presented with two tickets for
a "modern chamber music" concert. Despising this kind of an
evening and hating to waste the tickets, Posci offers them to his
subordinate Moscopasca, who is very moved and accepts them
for his daughter Titi and himself. But Moscopasca doesn't have
an evening dress and so he cannot be Titi's escort. Posci, glad to
be rid of the importunate Leo, sends him as the escort.

In Act II, Leo enters Moscopasca's house as Toons' son. His
intention is to swindle as much money as possible and disappear,
but when he meets Titi, shy, excited, pretty, and ashamed of her

remade evening dress, he sympathizes with her plight and her wish for a different life; feeling attracted to her, he renounces his scheme. Titi dreams of a life which doesn't include a firemen's ball, where she went last time she went out with her boyfriend Bernardo. She tells how at that ball she felt "unhappy among those vulgar, happy people, that music...."[53] Leo responds that we all have "wings" which, if the occasion arises, will enable us to fly. When they remain alone for the first time, he toasts "a land that certainly does exist...where everyone, everyone! has...his share of happiness waiting for him! A land, I don't know if to the South, to the North, to the West, to the East...."[54] Of course, the audience realizes that Titi's escape will never become a reality; his words remind us of the fairytale kingdom East of the sun and West of the moon.

Posci arrives and tries to dissuade Leo from impersonating young Toons, but Leo, realizing that Posci would be complicitous in his impersonation, doesn't reveal himself. Instead he asks for a tin tiara made by Toons and Son Co. for his date. Posci goes to get it, and when he comes back with old Toons himself, Titi and Leo exit through the back door. They don't go to the concert but to the Jasmine café which, as Titi tells him, is "a most beautiful place where rich people go. All the poor girls before they fall asleep, imagine that some night they will find themselves there with someone like you [Leo]."[55]

At the café, where Act III takes place, Titi and the penniless Leo drink champagne, order caviar and lobster; Leo buys a whole basket of flowers. Almost in love with Titi he tries to tell her the truth, but she doesn't believe him; she thinks he is trying to test her. Leo tries to convince her that happiness is not in the elegance of café life, that she is wrong and stupid not to understand the joy of family life, and not to cherish Bernardo's love. If she doesn't believe it, she is "the most stupid and hateful person in the world."[56] She cries. Meanwhile Bernardo arrives to rescue her. Old Toons, Posci, and Titi's parents also arrive. Leo tries to explain that "happiness is something that everyone carries in his pocket."[57] Everyone leaves except Leo, but, in the last scene, Titi comes back and apologizes. Leo gives her the tiara to wear on her wedding day with Bernardo.

This is a better comedy than *A Beautiful September Sunday*. Adriana is too petty and serious to escape her circumstances, even into the lightness of a smile; Titi is less sensible and certainly not as lyrical as Adriana. One is supposed to be, and perhaps one is, moved by Adriana's envy of the red-faced servant girls in that they represent youth and happiness; Titi's aspirations are much more concrete in spite of Leo's "lyrical" language and talk about "wings." It is a question for her of flying from the firemen's ball and what it represents to the elegant world represented by the Jasmine café — champagne, caviar, and other expensive food and drink. Titi is indeed a "dilettante" whose head, in an Emma Bovaryan way, is "full of movies."[58] But if the audience is less moved by Titi than by Adriana, it is more attracted to Titi: it can even smile at her.

Leo is also a more ingratiating character than Carlo. In his comical way Leo is a real outsider both when he plays the role of Toons' son and as himself. His attraction for Titi is more genuine and believable than Carlo's for Adriana. He sees through Titi's phony aspiration, and is forced to renounce his own phoniness, which on the stage is very comical; Titi's refusal to accept the truth enhances the comedy of the situation.

There are two reasons why *Our Dreams* is much less heavy-handed than *A Beautiful September Sunday*. One is that he is dealing with a social class lower than his own; the other is the situation itself which doesn't require the breakup of a marriage but, at the most, a not-yet official understanding. At the end of the play, there is even a hint that this understanding may be broken, since Titi comes back with something like "an offer,"[59] which Leo does not accept. It is not surprising that the public reacted more warmly to Titi and Leo than to Adriana and Carlo. Adriana's marriage, of course, could not be broken, for this would have meant tragedy for Betti. It is difficult if not impossible, to make light comedy of something one deems sacred.

V. Favola di Natale

In Betti's fourth and last comedy, *Favola di Natale* (1937;

Christmas Fable), an engagement is broken between Adalberto and Marta who are going to get married not out of love but for convenience. When his friend Antonio asks him if he is in love with Marta, Adalberto replies: "You are living in prehistory."[60] And when Antonio asks Marta: "Do you really love him madly?" she retorts: "Whom?" When Antonio explains he means her fiancé, she, who has been trying to hide all her twenty-eight years, sighs: "Ah. My God. He is so dear, Adalberto."[61] Because of such unseriousness the engagement will be called off, and Marta will marry Antonio instead of Adalberto. Theirs will be a perfect marriage. It will represent what a critic calls, "Bettian conjugal love."[62] In fact, Marta states: "Above all, I would really like to have my own house, full of things...and someone...who would scold me, and preach at me...."[63] Antonio's ideal is that a man should protect his woman "from everybody and everything, for all her life."[64] Two such characters cannot provoke laughter for long.

For the third time in four comedies a café represents "escape." Here Antonio sees Marta and convinces Adalberto to leave her. By the end Marta and Antonio realize they are in love with one another. The comic moments in this play are very few, and some are forced and conventional, as the author himself was aware. G.H. McWilliam, who studied these minor plays in detail, notes that in this comedy Betti's "vein of comic inspiration had definitely run dry."[65]

Chapter 4

In the Dark Wood

> *But where danger is, there*
> *Arises salvation also* (*Hölderlin*, Patmos).

I. Notte in casa del ricco

In Betti's next play, *Notte in casa del ricco* (1938; *Night in the Rich Man's House*), there is no trace of the light tone of the preceding four comedies. That these were merely escapist, outside the mainstream of Betti's theater, is suggested by the fact that in this play the author seems to pick up where he had left off four years before in *The Duck Hunter*. In the last scene of that play the conflict is between "dark chaos" and the hoped-for justice that the Regent will eventually bring. The Prologue of *Night in the Rich Man's House* throbs with the anguished question of whether the lives of human beings are determined by chance or whether a logical thread can be perceived to run through them.

The Prologue takes place in the waiting room of a small railroad station set in a low valley, after the last night train has left. In silence, solitude, and darkness Betti succeeds in suspending ordinary time and space, both for the audience and for the characters. We are not surprised that Mauro and Tito feel free,

48

almost compelled, to reveal their innermost feelings and secrets. It is as if in this suspended condition the two uncover their souls; as if they uttered to each other those nightmares they would have dreamt had they been able to sleep. As individuals they are strangers to one another, but nightmare is collective and unites them. Without any preamble, without any introduction, Tito impulsively confesses that he is chained to his life. He expresses a wish to climb onto a train, any train, go to a faraway city, and change everything. But it is impossible to leave one's own actions behind: "A fact that ends, passes, we could even forget it. But, this act...which is not there any longer...continues to stay there worse than a stone.... It changes shape as if not to be recognized, and it forces us,...it forces us."[1] Jumping on a train and acquiring a new existence is impossible. Some actions cannot be annihilated, they are part of one's past and one's future. "Action — R.D. Laing writes — is the dead end of possibility. It scleroses freedom."[2] Tito has committed a deed which will always be the incubus of his life; in fact, his observation — "it changes shape as if not to be recognized" — poignantly reveals that a deed is not just a deed but an unalterable destiny. Even if this destiny is "chance. Evil chance."[3] It is not a question of morality but of being. When Mauro suggests to him that he is feeling remorse, Tito denies it: "I meant something else: consequences.... As if an evil force forces me to go down a certain road, necessary, between two walls."[4] He doesn't feel guilty in the sense that he has behaved badly; his anguish derives from being condemned *to be* that action, as in a Dantean hell; in the words of Heidegger: "'One is' what one does."[5] He has seduced Amelia, the young daughter of his employer Valerio; he has taken advantage of her innocence and inexperience; now she despises him, and he suffers for it, but they cannot do without one another: sensual impulses dominate their lives.

For Mauro facts are not important, because he is old and he feels he will die "very soon." Since he has no future, he is not chained to the past. He says: "I reached the end of my life, almost without realizing it."[6] Near death, he is awakened to life, in the existentialist sense that death awakens him into a consciousness of the meaning of his life. The reason for his travelling is the desire to expose the friend of his youth, Valerio. As young men they stole, but Valerio succeeded in avoiding punishment while Mauro went to jail. He has heard that Valerio, now very rich and respected, is about to be honored as city councilman, and Mauro cannot accept the absurdity of chance on which their lives depended. It is not envy that moves him, nor is it justice; again, as for Tito, it is not a question of moral exigency that concerns Mauro, it is an ontological quest. He says: "It is not injustice that stirs me. It is disharmony. Do you understand? Does only chance direct us?"[7] To die with the secret of Valerio buried in him means passively accepting an inharmonious universe. His act is the only way he knows of redeeming himself and the universe: by correcting only one discrepancy in it. He will not go gentle into that good night. His last words, before they get up to leave, are: "I had to make this trip to be tranquil and serene in the moment when I will turn my back on all of this."[8]

Dawn arrives and nightmares end. After talking to each other of the most intimate details of their lives, they have not become friends; they confessed to each other, they didn't communicate. At times, while talking, it seems they are not even together; instead of answering each other, they just continue to speak of their own pain; like all human beings, they cannot control their nightmares. It is as if they were trying to overpower one another, like the characters in *Six Characters in Search of an Author*. Tito and Mauro are monads, they suffer at the same time and with the same intensity but not together. Betti underlines this monadic state, for twice Mauro ends a line with this remark: "It is for this reason I started the trip."[9] Both times Tito retorts by speaking of Adelia. First, "The girl despises me"; then, "The girl...the girl whom I was talking to you about...." As one critic observes, in this Prologue "as in Greek tragedy, the antefact is presented and it shares with Greek tragedy that sense of a grandiose fatality, of a superior justice which dominates events."[10] Like Tito and Mauro, the other two main characters of the play are also uncommunicating monads, Valerio and his daughter Adelia.

All three acts take place in Valerio's house. A delegation has come from town to ask Valerio to be city councilman. Before he appears we learn from the members of the delegation that he has always kept himself apart. "He has become strangely rich; he is strangely hard, strangely honest, strangely solitary and he has also been good, strangely good."[11] They respect him for his power and riches, and one of them, Antonio, asks him if his son can call on his daughter. Valerio for the first time realizes Adelia is not a little girl. The visit is interrupted when, alerted by the dogs' barking, they find Mauro in the garden. When he is brought in, he admires Adelia's beauty and notices her pallor; he also greets Tito, who is Valerio's secretary. The visitors, thinking he is just a vagrant, are about to send him away, but Adelia asks her father to allow him to spend the night since it is already dark. Valerio, who has recognized him, consents and offers him the wooden hut at the edge of the garden.

In the second act, Valerio remains alone and opens the door to the garden knowing Mauro will want to speak to him; in fact Mauro is standing near the door. Valerio faces his past in Mauro, and Mauro, in Valerio, faces his moment of liberation from chance by rectifying a distortion in the world. In the second scene again two characters confess their desperation. Valerio offers Mauro anything he wants; he will make him rich if he will not use the evidence he is carrying to expose him. When Mauro refuses, Valerio perceives that Mauro's motivation has deeper roots. The motivation is not greed, and it is not envy. Valerio feels that he must deal with Mauro on a different level, on one that must involve the larger question of good and evil, and the rationality of existence, not just their own personal histories – one escaping justice and the other being caught, and paying for both of them.

Valerio then begins the play's longest monologue: "Listen, Mauro. There is one thing that you don't know and that nobody knows."[12] This second act, in fact, has the same atmosphere of the Prologue: it is night, the two characters are alone, and Mauro's presence evokes the nightmarish past which accompanies Valerio's "free" life. He tells Mauro that it is not true that God was unjust; his life has been a life sentence, condemned first to fear, then to hate. Since he projected his own "poison" into everyone he knew, all his life he has remained an outsider. It seems as if he has never spoken to anyone "with simplicity, with trust." Perhaps he has not been what he should have been, even with his daughter. He asks himself why that mistake, almost forgotten, has ruined his life. "Why did I waste my life?"[13]

Yet, in spite of this confession, there is no more communication here than in the Prologue; they are not able to comprehend each other. Valerio says that he feels he has wasted his life; the statement should make Mauro, whose life was also ruined, feel kinship with him; but when Valerio asks him again what he wants, Mauro answers that he wants his own life back: "I want Mauro."[14] This creates the most intense moment in the play. In fact, they both are at the end of their lives: "I feel...full of weariness," Valerio says. Both realize their lives are and were without meaningful direction, but their desperation divides them even more. Mauro's answer—"I want Mauro"—reveals to himself, to Valerio, and to the audience the anguish of the irrevocability of time. This is the climax of the play; there is no harmony; there is no brotherhood of men symbolized by "Pity," as in *Landslide*; no hope for an afterlife of meaning symbolized by a Regent, as in *The Duck Hunter*. Men are starkly alone. Mauro, and through him Betti, doesn't see any possible reconciliation, and that is why Mauro asks Valerio for Adelia, knowing it is impossible.

The *dénouement* of Act III underscores the play's climax in failing to achieve universal harmony. Instead of just stealing the incriminating documents as Valerio asks, Tito kills Mauro by firing the hut where Mauro sleeps. His plan is to blackmail his master into allowing him to marry his daughter. But since her shameful relation to Tito has been discovered, Adelia poisons herself, although her father has understood and forgiven, and is willing to help her. The four individuals cannot communicate, and man cannot bring the heavenly music of the spheres into his own world. "Facts cannot be erased,"[15] wrote Betti in his notes.

Night in the Rich Man's House is one of Betti's most balanced plays, with the intimacy of the confessional Prologue followed by a crowded and active Act I, then again the intimacy of revelation in Act II, and at the end another crowded and eventful final act. Perhaps an apt subtitle would be "Nightmares in the Rich Man's House."

II. Il vento notturno

The wind in the title of *Il vento Notturno* (1941; *The Night Wind*) is a childhood reminiscence of Antonio, one of the play's two protagonists. Often Betti uses childhood to symbolize the desire to return to a state of innocence and freshness. For Antonio, childhood is not just a sentimental memory which he would like to relive since he is approaching old age, as Commendatore La Quarta, his boss, interprets it; childhood had been a presence during Antonio's entire life, a presence as the *autre* of his existence, and Antonio would have continued to a quietly desperate old age without moment. He lives with his mother in an apartment house; a wall — with a door now always kept locked — separates his living room and bedroom from the living room of the apartment where Elisa and Pietro, who have been lovers for ten years, live. Pietro tries to make ends meet by not entirely legal means and abuses Elisa every day; she accuses him of having ruined her life. But they cannot leave each other. Their screaming and fighting are the scandal of the building.

When the other tenants want to petition the owner to evict them, Antonio, the most important tenant, defends them. Everyone believes he is infatuated with Elisa. Although she has never seen him and he has never tried to approach her, Elisa also believes he is interested in her, just as any other man who meets her would be. In fact, he even phones to tell Pietro not to abuse her when she and Pietro start screaming at each other. She is glad of this attention and even starts thinking of a better life. But when, at the end of Act I, she finds out from the maid that he is old enough to be her father, she becomes angry, thinking mistakenly he is just a lecherous old man.

During the first act, time is measured by the noise of unimportant events and by the conversation of daily routine: mothers calling their children, the high cost of stringbeans, the distribution of the mail, gossip. It is pertinent that when Antonio steps upon the stage for the first time, at the end of the first scene, "almost at the same time" one hears the scream of the milkman, "Milk! Milk!" and the sound of his trumpet.[16]

The triviality which confronts Antonio at his first appearance is a symbol of, and a reminder of, a life filled with pettiness and loneliness. He would *have lived* and would live another life with at least some intensity and with the contact of another human being. So, when some evenings his neighbors scream, fight, and *live*, he vicariously lives with and through them. He has become fond especially of Elisa's little girl who usually, after her parents stop fighting, can be heard singing softly. It is for her that he saved them from eviction. The audience is privy to this affection; so a certain suspension has been built up by the end of Act I, when again we hear the milkman's voice and trumpet.

In Act II Elisa goes to Antonio's office, perhaps to seduce him, but also wishing to unburden herself of her suffering, her disgust and spite for Pietro, who seduced her when she was eighteen while his wife was dying. She asks Antonio for help so that she can leave her lover. Suddenly Pietro arrives and the two make a scene before him, and it becomes clear that both are victims of their neurotic attachment to each other. This scene and all of the second act remind us of Pirandello's *It Is So (If You Think So)* and *Each in His Own Way*.[17]

After Pietro leaves, Antonio protests his disinterested and honest intentions; Elisa is bewildered and sad because she really does need somebody since she says she is alone in the world. Antonio inquires about her little girl who sings so sadly, and Elisa explains that there is no one, that she herself sings in a falsetto voice.

Antonio's gentle misunderstanding doesn't console her and she leaves, angered. Elisa, infuriated once again at Pietro, tells him that from now on she can leave him whenever she wants and go to her newly found father...Antonio. In the following scene Pietro tells Antonio that his pure attentions to Elisa have shocked her into the delusion that he, Antonio, is her father. Antonio reacts as if it were a blackmailing scheme, and Pietro shouts at him: "Even if she were a prostitute, Elisa would be cleaner than you with all your honesty."[18] Again the spectators witness a new and surprising view of the relation between Pietro and Elisa. He speaks of his concern for her, for after they fight and he runs out, he imagines that she may really have thrown herself out of a window — her customary threat — and he hurries back because, as he says: "I don't care what Elisa is, it is enough that on going back and on opening the door, I hear her in the other room alive, alive. I spit on the rest."[19] He adds that: "Perhaps one should have been...loving, respectful, with her."[20]

The next scene of the play, in which Elisa visits Antonio in his apartment, is a pivotal point and the most delicate and poignant part of the play. Up to now it has been more or less a "modest, bourgeois, and romantic reverie."[21] Now Betti moves, in Gioacchino Pellecchia's words, "into a sphere of intense lyricism, filled with deep and far-reaching echoes and references."[22] The scene uncannily represents a psychic line between consciousness and the unconscious. It seems as if Antonio and Elisa are speaking — even experiencing themselves — as two different persons; or, to speak in Pirandellian terms, it seems as if each person is projecting or living another character. Elisa and Antonio face each other in their own right; *they know* who they are, yet at the same time, subconsciously, they treat one another, not as father and daughter, as in a sentimental play, but believing, and behaving as if, they are father and daughter, affectionately, lovingly. Only at the end of the scene do they seem to come out of the trance; Elisa "*suddenly and absolutely disconcerted, silently stretches out her arms toward Antonio and whispers*: 'My God. My God,'" and runs away. Antonio alone in the room, as if awakened "*suddenly screams*: 'But no, no, what are you thinking...what folly....'"[23]

Moments after, two gun shots are heard from Elisa's and Pietro's apartment. Several neighbors, afraid one of the two may be dead, come into Antonio's apartment to break down the connecting door. When it is forced open, Pietro comes out saying that everything is fine; he was just cleaning his gun and it went off. When everyone leaves, he tells Antonio that Elisa has tried to kill him, and that she is now very sick and desperate. Before he goes, Antonio suggests to him: "Tell her I am her father. She really believes it. And you tell her it is true."[24]

This is a scene which brings real life to the stage. Betti has succeeded in having his two protagonists create for themselves a magic "spot in time"; one critic writes that "the play acquires a fairy tale tone; the man ends up by recognizing Elisa as his daughter."[25] From such a "spot" they can exist but only at the expense of their normal lives, like the three main characters of the play *It Is So (If You Think So)* or the one protagonist of *Henry IV*. In fact, in the first scene of Act III Antonio is able to tell his superior that nothing he has done up to now in his life interests him; he would like "to hear once again the mountain wind" as he used to as a child before he was encumbered by "duty"; he is trying to carve a new *Lebensraum*: he doesn't even want to see his mother and leaves a moment before Elisa enters. His mother, Candida, cuts through Elisa's pretense with candor; she forces her to admit that she doesn't *really* believe she is Antonio's daughter or that Antonio *really* thinks he is her father. Elisa runs away crying. Signora Ponza of *It Is So (If You Think So)* would have reacted differently by continuing to pretend; 'Henry IV' also reacts differently when people discover he is pretending to be mad by killing, so that he may have the right to be mad forever.

Pathos is maintained by accepting strife forever or by succumbing to destiny. However, in the last scene the play descends from the height of impossibility to the experience of possibility when Elisa climbs onto the terrace of the building. She has decided to jump to her death; the deed would bring a realistic tone to the lyricism of the second act, but still it would keep the terror of tragedy. But Antonio, instead of failing to arrive on time and jumping after Elisa or screaming at the gods, arrives in time to convince her to continue living: "You will leave [the tenement] tomorrow, we will not see each other any more. But...some beautiful day, certainly, we will find each other again.... Over there we will be happy, gay.... All the things we ask for will be true, do you understand? There Elisa will go arm in arm with her father."[26] This "transcendental solution"[27] has the characteristic of a *deus ex machina*; it is too easy or at least the spectator feels that Elisa is too easily and too quickly converted.

III. Marito e moglie

Marito e moglie (1942–1943; *Husband and Wife*) recapitulates many of Betti's concerns that appeared in his previous writing. Among the most visible of them: first, the motif of *tempus fugit*, life unlived, unloved daily routine; second, the recollection of childhood as a desire for rebirth, as evidence of the unbearableness of the present, the incommunicability of human beings, the difficulty of being sincere with oneself and others; third, the discovery, in the face of the otherworldly, of the truth of one's own feelings, the possibility of communicating and the hope of "another" life full of happiness in the eternity of time, where, perhaps, there is a God.

Each of this three-part division of Bettian concerns corresponds to one of the three acts of *Husband and Wife*. Indeed, Betti uses a different style for each of the acts, and this mixing of artistic approaches may be perceived as a break in the rhythm of the composition. One critic dismisses this play as "of rather minor poetic worth, above all for the uncertainty of expressive forms, which reveal too much incoherence between the first and the third act: very beautiful, but too different and isolated."[28] Another critic notices "in the action a progression disproportionate and without gradation, from the Sunday picnic (in Act I) to the investigation of the husband's subconscious."[29] But there is one critic, Ruggero Jacobbi, who believes that Betti constructed the play "deliberately according to three different techniques, one for each act."[30] Aside from the question of whether this is a successful method or not—in twentieth century Italian literature, Lampedusa's *Leopard*, written in different styles, is a positive example—we agree with Jacobbi's statement.

In fact each act can also be compared, *per similia* or *per dissimilia*, with some preceding plays. The first act repeats, as has already been observed,[31] the atmosphere of *Summertime*, which Betti seems to have been revising for its première just before beginning work on *Husband and Wife*. The setting of Act I is, as in *Summertime*, outdoors, a picnic by the sea. A group of friends are enjoying the summer day, but now the pleasure is shadowed by an undertone of sadness whose cause is the distortion of "healthy" feelings. Luigi's relation to his wife, Olga, is neurotic— he is master, teacher, tamer, and she is a little girl completely dependent on him. He says to Carletto, a childhood friend he hasn't seen for years: "I had a great influence on her.... Before doing anything, she glances at me, instinctively, poor devil, as if she were asking my permission."[32] He also confesses that at times he feels a certain melancholy, but when his friend inquires why, he retorts: "But no, no motive. Because actually I am very happy."[33]

At the picnic, a neighbor, Erminia, is also present, whose attachment to her twenty year old nephew, Filippo, is also morbid. Filippo is infatuated with Olga, and his aunt tries to seduce her for him. When Olga tells her he is just like a baby, like her two year old Corradino, Erminia, like a modern day insinuating Celestina, answers: "It is beautiful to feel oneself searched by the hot and bad hands of babies."[34] In her next lines she says, alluding to Filippo: "I cannot bear thinking that bad, dirty women may get near him."[35] In words that could be uttered by Fyodor Karamazov, she tells herself: "I don't care anything of Paradise or of her [Olga]. I want my Filippo to be well and happy."[36] Of course this is only her apparent motivation, for the real one must be seen as vicarious incestuous pleasure.

Carletto is obsessed with the thought that perhaps the pain in his stomach will end his life, and "in two or three months [he] will have to say farewell to everything, trees, moon, people, etc...."[37] Indeed, in Act III the audience will learn that he suffered from an incurable disease and that he died a few months after. This character is not just a sentimental note; his physical sickness is a reflection of the falsehood in the psyches of Luigi, Olga, and Erminia. In fact, this symbolism of physical illness is underlined by another character's physical abnormality. Signorina Giulia is "very slightly lame." She is also the first character in the play to use a stage technique Betti introduces for the first time. Wanting to make public his characters' thoughts, he lets them speak out, for as Betti explains at the beginning of the play, "if thoughts are really thoughts, that is, something unmistakably intimate, this will be sufficient to distinguish them from ordinary lines."[38]

Most of Act II makes use of this new technique. In the fourth and fifth scenes Luigi and Olga confront one another; Olga would like to go downstairs and say goodby to Filippo, for at five o'clock he will go out and she will not be able to see him again. The next day he will leave for Torino. She is not in love with Filippo, but she is flattered by his attentions, and she is excited to be part of his youthful sensations and thoughts, especially now that she is entering middle age. But Luigi is jealous and prohibits her going. The words they exchange are polite, gentle, even loving. Olga speaks of when she was a little girl, Luigi of the fact that even if he has not had a brilliant career, they are doing well anyhow. But their thinking, which the audience can hear, reveals what they say to themselves and what they really would like to say to each other. In contrast with their words, their thoughts are not polite but rude, not gentle but cruel, not loving but hateful. Their thoughts reveal what their words are meant to hide from one another — the state of their unhappiness and frustration, their lack of spiritual intimacy, the anger of lives without satisfaction. Olga resents having been coerced into a child-like existence, regrets her loss of youth, and despairs at the thought that she will become old. That is why she keeps talking of when she was a pretty little girl, almost as an invocation to start her life anew. The approach of middle age means for her the approach of death. She seems to beg for more life as she stares at the light of sunset entering through the window and which slowly creeps away from the cupboard to the painting on the wall. She keeps saying: "Where are you going. Dear longed-for light?"[39] When she thinks of old age, in contrast to the conciliating Adriana of *A Beautiful September Sunday*, Olga screams to herself: "My God. Old. Help. Help."[40]

Luigi's thoughts reveal his fear of being alone, his self-hatred, and his hatred of Olga for not being happy. He knows he is being cruel to her in not letting her bid goodbye to young Filippo; he wants her with him, and he continues to talk about their son Corradino as if to remind her of her family duties. A most powerful and grotesque moment in the scene comes after Olga translates her husband's talk of Corradino as a message meaning: "Be good, Olga, be good, let yourself be put into the coffin, think of Corradino."[41] After these words Luigi, who is binding a book, makes a thudding sound, but Olga thinks it is the sound of a nail driven into her coffin:

"Luigi: (*strikes*)
Olga: Corradino.
Luigi: (*strikes*)
Olga: Corradino."[42]

Luigi is glad she is losing her youth and beauty so that she cannot leave him. But he is also conscious that he is acting as a jailer. Within himself, he asks her forgiveness and decides to go out for the evening so that she will be free to see Filippo. The act ends with Olga saying to herself: "I only want to laugh with him.... I will stay a minute. Only one minute."[43]

That minute becomes a year, if not an eternity. Act III takes place one year later in a tribunal. Olga and Filippo were surprised in intimacy by the servant girl, Irma, who out of jealousy started screaming in the stairwell of the tenement and describing what she saw to the tenants who would listen. Olga wanted to rush to her apartment but, ashamed by the people on the stairs, left the building and never came back. Later, Luigi also left town and nobody saw him anymore. After his wife left, he hired a lawyer, Ricci, to get custody of Corradino.

At the beginning of the third act Betti wants to give the audience the impression of mystery. Ricci suggests that after Luigi left "one could say that the thing [the court procedure] continued by itself; only by itself."[44] Some of the characters—like Olga's sister and Irene—apparently come to court inexpectedly. Some of them, one critic notices, "even lose their own names, their social dress, the first moment they appear, and are reduced to sounds, unknown entities, which slowly coagulate and reveal their precedent reality"[45]; so it happens with Olga's sister and, to a certain extent, with Luigi. By the end of the act there is a shift, in characteristically Bettian fashion, from a realistic to a surreal plane; to this change in artistic mode there corresponds a shift from societal to universal concerns, from the worldy to the otherwordly. Luigi seems to underline the difference when he observes: "I also brought the child. We could not keep away, it is too important, for us. (*Brief pause*). Maybe in the great universe it is a rather small question."[46]

The principal characters now appear stripped of the selfishness and hypocrisy they have shown in the preceding acts. In fact, the distinction between what they said and what they were thinking, which prevented communication, is abolished. Olga's and Luigi's words now express their thoughts. But complete honesty, frankness, and reconciliation are achieved only now, that is, in a rarefied atmosphere nearly otherwordly for Luigi; for Olga it is achieved only after death. Terror, at this point, is inspired by the realization of the impossibility of being oneself and of communicating with others. The fact that this can be achieved only outside the circumstances of existence adds pity and renders it tragic.

Nevertheless, this husband and wife are not tragic but pathetic characters. They too, like several other Bettian figures, hope to be saved in the afterlife. They both hope to be, as Luigi's last speech hints, "on a island, a beautiful island, like a leaf."[47] As the play ends, he says: "Now everything is explained."[48] Maybe it is true that for Luigi, and also for Olga, everything has been explained, but the spectator cannot be so easily won over because he has not seen the struggle necessary to achieve such a beatific state of grace. One critic believes that this ending "actually doesn't explain anything at all."[49] Of course, it is not that one needs an explanation but rather a struggle toward an explanation.

IV. Spiritismo nell'antica casa

With his next play, *Spiritismo nell'antica casa* (1943-1944; *Spiritism in the Ancient House*), it seems that Betti wants to resolve an impasse he has been living with for a long time. In *The Duck Hunter, The Night Wind,* and *Husband and Wife,* Betti's several protagonists have given meaning to their lives, or have mustered enough courage to bear the slings and arrows of outrageous fortune, or have experienced a condition of goodness and of love by positing an afterlife and at times even a God. There they will shed forever the ugliness of the present. Betti's religiosity and belief in the Christian God is the obvious source of the recurrence of such themes in his plays. However these plays are not religious in the same sense that Betti is. His characters are not Christian at all. One can say of them what one critic says of

Husband and Wife: "One reaches the need of transcendence not through ways which have the force of a clear conviction, but through the need of the heart's longing."[50] The same critic, Gildo Moro, speaks of lack of faith[51] in regard to *Spiritism in the Ancient House*.

It is this lack of faith in the characters that generates an intellectual impasse in Betti, the playwright. He can attribute to them a transcendent belief, but if this is not based, like his own, on the Christian faith, but on an existential "heart's" necessity, then his character must "leap" either into faith, with Kierkegaard, and consequently into eternity or directly into eternity by merely hoping for it; and if the hope is so strong as to be a belief, the character without faith may leap directly into eternity by jumping out of a window, as Enzo, the unbeliever of *Spiritism in the Ancient House*, argues; and as Laura, the weak co-protagonist, does.

It must be noticed that this is the first suicide of a main character in Betti's theater. Elena, in *The Duck Hunter*, is a very minor character who kills herself in a moment of desperation when abandoned by her lover Marco. But in fact, of the many unhappy and hopeless characters aware of their misery no one talks himself into suicide. On the contrary, Betti's most cynical character, Enzo, who is convinced of human baseness and of his own condition as the wreck of a hopelessly rotten body, not only doesn't commit suicide but clings, in the cynical and pessimistic materiality of flesh, even more fiercely and more desperately to his life exactly because that's all there is.[52] He would kill himself if he had the slightest hope in any kind of life after death, and he convinces Laura to witness her hope in a special place where she will be united with her beloved dead husband. But the match is uneven. Laura doesn't have a very developed reasoning. She seems to succumb to, not be convinced by, Enzo's argument.

Laura was traumatized three years before. At a railroad station her husband, Carlo, told her: "Wait for me a minute." He never came back; he was killed by a train. Like the minute Olga suffers at the end of Act II in *Husband and Wife*, Carlo's minute becomes an eternity. From earthly union and love at the outset, their relation will be felt as an event beyond contingency. Shocked for almost three years, Laura wandered, "a poor, painted, mad woman,"[53] in her heart still longing for Carlo's body and love. Tired in body and soul, she comes back to the ancient house where she had met him. Irma, Carlo's mother, and Enzo, her second husband, live here, also does Federica, Enzo's sister, very old and very rich, the owner of the house. In order to get away from the war raging through Italy she came with a young relative, the "depraved" Ruggero and a servant, Isolina. One evening (in Act I) they have a séance to distract themselves. A Professor, who visits with them every day and who is a great believer in spiritualism, states: "Death life, life death: only one great house where we live. Why don't we get used to walking freely, trust-fully? This side and that side."[54] Ruggero is the medium. Enzo just laughs, knowing Ruggero pretends. Laura has never partici-pated, but this evening she remains with them; during the séance she believes Carlo enters the room, and she becomes hysterical. The séance ends, but Laura asks Ruggero to continue tomorrow so she can be again with Carlo. At the end of the act, Enzo tells Ruggero the story of a widow in a nearby village: after her hus-band's death, she screamed for three or four days, then she calmed down and for years afterward she would set a place at the table everyday for him and would be heard speaking to him for hours.

Act II takes place a few days later. It starts with Isolina re-counting the same story of the widow. We learn that it is that time in the evening when Ruggero and Laura have a séance alone, and we witness it. Laura falls into a frenzy of sensual desire in the evocation of Carlo, while Ruggero, who takes voyeuristic plea-sure in watching her, envies her undying love and wishes to re-place Carlo. Finally an enraged Ruggero tells Laura the whole thing is a deception. He convinces her to love him in his real flesh and blood.

In Act III Ruggero and Laura prepare to leave, but before they do, Laura and Enzo, believer and disbeliever, confront one another. The play ends with Laura's "terrible, immense scream," while falling to her death, and with Enzo's comment, the last word of the play: "Victorious."[55]

We noticed that Enzo and Laura are not evenly matched. Like the widow of the nearby village—the story told twice in the play is meant as a comment on its protagonist—Laura is a traumatized creature with weak nerves, a morbid attachment to Carlo's memory, and an abnormal hypersensitiveness. She is too suggestible for anyone to claim that Enzo's argument has prevailed. But in spite of the unevenness of the two characters, the struggle they perform is not uneven but tragic. They each represent an individual condition hardly bearable and without solution of any kind. He is aware of the hopelessness of his finitude in the face of death. She, less aware, but equally and desperately feeling the pulsations of the physicality of life, the train, Carlo's wrecked body, her own body, struggles not to accept finitude by hoping for a metaphysical existence. Enzo and Laura are the obverse of one another. Enzo might possibly avoid his condition by converting to Laura's belief; Laura could renounce her hope and become a cynic like Enzo. There is no other choice. The only act which will allow man to prevail over his despair and bestow freedom is a leap into death. This is the meaning of the play's last word, "Victorious." Enzo means that Laura wins whether she is right or wrong. It is a very poor victory, but the only one. Perhaps Laura's act is too "theatrical" and symbolic,[56] but most of the play is theatrical, especially the séance, which together with Laura's near-madness prepares the audience for the apparently improbable last act.

It is difficult to agree completely with Di Pietro's interpretation of Laura's scream as expressing "Betti's revolt against a state of desperate confusion...that dark historical moment...[when] Italy [was] run by foreign armies...and torn apart by civil war."[57] Only later in his career will Betti show a certain interest in social and political themes.

V. Corruzione al Palazzo di Giustizia

Corruzione al Palazzo di Giustizia (1944; *Corruption in the Palace of Justice*, 1962) is considered by many critics Betti's greatest play. One of them, for example, writes: "I think that one must start with *Corruption* to fix a valid basis for understanding all of Betti's world."[58] Clearly the play is a most representative Bettian creation. Its structure is the most typical and successful the author makes use of, the investigation. The play also focuses on some quite frequent, almost obsessive, concerns: justice, guilt, loss of innocence, and the desire to atone.

It is customary to compare this play to *Landslide* in regard to style and theme. Each is an investigation into a crime: in each play guilt is not limited to the one actually responsible for the crime but to the whole society; in each the investigation, besides discovering the criminal, fathoms the privacy of man's soul; each is a "metaphysical detective story," as one critic calls *Corruption in the Palace of Justice*.[59] In each there is a self-condemnation not condemnation. And one may in part apply to *Landslide* what Betti wrote about *Corruption in the Palace of Justice*: "In spite of everything,...the unsuppressible need for justice and the absolute ends by triumphing in the depth of the human soul.... This is...the thesis of my play."[60]

But beyond these obvious and valid similarities there are differences which make the two plays quite diverse works of art. In *Landslide* Betti shows more originality in his effective use of stage devices; especially impressive is his ability in the theatrically believable presentation of dead people on stage. Another difference is that *Landslide* is based on a chorality of feeling while *Corruption in the Palace of Justice* is based mainly on the struggle of one individual. The endings divide the two plays drastically: *Landslide* remains within the earthly "desert": *Corruption in the Palace of Justice* seems to invoke an extra-human sphere. As in *The Duck Hunter*, the existence of a higher being is implied, the Alto Revisore (The Supreme Judge). Gino Rizzo, who interprets the play in a key of Catholic symbolism, suggests that "The teleology of *Landslide* left a gap between the sphere of the human and the sphere of the divine that could only be filled through the Incarnation. This is the gap Betti fills in *Corruption in the Palace of Justice*."[61]

These two plays are not the only ones with an inspection or trial—most, even if not officially, concern investigation. The fact that the author was a professional judge is the outward explanation for his choice of this artistic method in the composition of these plays. But the inner reason for the choice is more complex.

One must not forget that Betti was a Roman Catholic and not in the superficial sense that he was Italian and born Catholic; he was a very religious believer, and as such, he was forever obsessed by injustice and by evil in the heart of man. It was this continuous questing that made the investigative method his natural manner of composition.

And if the professional magistrate had some influence on the professional playwright, the playwright's imagination seems to have influenced the magistrate's attitude. Some sentences Betti published in a magazine for jurists could be placed as an introduction to many of his dramas. Silvio D'Amico, in fact, quotes them in his Introduction to Betti's *Teatro completo*: "There is in a place in the city a palace through whose door, everyday, the most varied people enter like a river: the strangest conditions, the most different dress.... There they scream, cry, lie, pronounce disconsolate, or atrocious, or fearful words."[62] In quoting the passage D'Amico has not noticed a very interesting parallel with the Preface to *Six Characters in Search of an Author* wherein Pirandello states that his "Fantasy...amuses herself by bringing to my house...the most disgruntled tribe in the world, men, women, children, involved in strange adventures...; thwarted in their plans; cheated in their hopes."[63] So the courthouse (sublimated in the artist's fantasy) brought his characters to Betti. Every play depicting an investigation is lifted from its realistic setting, and "in the foreground there is not the materiality of fact but its tragic vibration."[64]

Landslide has a realistic beginning, but "from its first lines [*Corruption*] comes alive in that suggestive atmosphere of nightmare, obsession, and death which circulates throughout the whole drama."[65] Right from the start, the audience witnesses the spectacle of six judges all of whom fear the inquest, and each other; all six having something dishonest to hide; all six trying to defend themselves; all six corrupt. It is not necessary to find a realistic explanation for this overwhelming fear. One critic thinks it appears abstract and "cerebral, unless one conceives of it in a totalitarian regime,"[66] and that "to understand...the dramatic situation one must consider it in an atmosphere without political freedom; otherwise the tragic atmosphere will seem arbitrary, forced and the characters cumbersome mannequins."[67] It is indeed pertinent to speculate about the political situation of accusation and counteraccusation, of cowards and informers, which characterized the time of the drafting of the play. Di Pietro has found in Betti's notes the author's intention of writing a drama about "a trial of political oppression"[68] in an ambience of the "cowardice...[of] ex-Fascists and of the purge."[69] But the intention was not translated into the play; the artist won over the injured individual—Betti also ran the possibility of being accused of Fascism at this time, in spite of the fact that during Fascism he had been accused of being both Jewish and anti-Fascist. *In Corruption in the Palace of Justice* there does remain something of the original intention, but quite sublimated and at the service of Betti's real interest: the investigation of the human being. A specific trace of an event which took place during the play's composition, the mutilating of Mussolini's corpse, are the lines about a dead man's body: "Let the body at least be only for the worms for whom all faces are equal."[70] "There is in these words a pitiless criticism of a society which, just when Betti was writing the drama, had reached a degrading incivility and inhumanity."[71]

Despite such political allusion, one can give a different, nonrealistic explanation for the "abstract" and "cerebral" fear, for the "arbitrary, forced" atmosphere, and for the characters' resemblance to "cumbersome mannequins,"—unrealistic elements which do characterize the beginning of *Corruption in the Palace of Justice*. The author took pains in presenting something beyond the pale of realism so that the play would not be perceived in the ordinary mode of everyday events. That all six judges are corrupt must indicate something besides the corruption of human justice or of society as a whole. One is justified in looking for another vision by the preceding dramas, where social and political concerns were always secondary or nonexistent. In *Corruption in the Palace of Justice* as in the preceding plays, Betti wants to investigate man in the absolute, not as a mere member of society.

The six corrupt judges are not meant to be a special case of human evil; they represent every man in his post-lapsarian condition. Betti finds himself "in a dark wood," outside of Eden, living the corruptibility of the soul and the decomposition of the body; only in the Garden is there no old age or death. So in the first lines of the play, the first piece of information Erzi, the investigating magistrate, is given is that Croz, the First Judge, has been "moribund for many months."[72] A few lines later, Erzi also discovers that in the Palace of Justice there is the smell of a decomposing body. The Employee says: "There must be some dead rat in some corner."[73] Later on, in the first act, the corpse of Ludvi-Pol is discovered in the palace. Moreover, as if to underline the condition of exile from the Garden, the Employee, again on the first page, calls the palace a "real labyrinth." Like Dante in the "dark wood," one finds oneself in the labyrinth where "The straight way *is* lost." The Employee is the Archivist who, because his task is filing documents, jokingly thinks of himself as a gravedigger. In the course of the play other direct and indirect references to man's post-lapsarian condition can be found. The investigation about to take place is not simply to discover the one responsible for the corruption. Indeed, from the outset the audience is presented with corrupt and guilty men, and by the end of the first act we already know the one responsible for the crime in question.

In fact, as soon as it is known that there is going to be an investigation and that Erzi is the investigator, we discover that everyone is guilty. As the investigator, Erzi represents self-scrutiny not scrutiny, self-discovery not discovery; his presence is the epiphanic moment in which every man can repeat "I found myself in a dark wood." But if everyone is capable, not everyone is able and courageous enough to undertake the analysis into self-consciousness and self-knowledge, the journey *ad inferos* necessary for rebirth. *Corruption* is the struggle through such a journey by one man, Cust.

The story of *Corruption in the Palace of Justice* appears straightforward. A powerful and important man, Ludvi-Pol, who is suspected of dirty dealing in high places is about to be questioned by the court when the documents the police were to seize were destroyed in a fire in which an innocent woman lost her life. The only people aware of the documents and the proceedings against Ludvi-Pol are the six members of the investigating

Council of Judges; one of them must be responsible for revealing the secret and must be involved with the swindler Ludvi-Pol. The citizenry is aware of the scandal and demands an inquiry. Erzi is sent to investigate. Each of the judges is afraid that his own dishonest deeds will be discovered; each one tries to defend himself and accuse a colleague. Since at their first meeting, Vanaan, President of the Council, is absent, the others find it convenient and easy to join against him. Vanaan is a very old man about to retire, once very handsome, now still a majestic figure with a powerful voice. When he arrives and finds out that he is a suspect, he loses his self-assurance, for he too has something to hide; in fact he once accepted money from Ludvi-Pol. He is so afraid that he is unable to defend himself. And Ludvi-Pol cannot be interrogated, his body has just been found in the building, perhaps a suicide. Judge Cust, the real culprit, the most intelligent and most scheming of the six, insinuates to Vanaan that the best thing for him to do is offer his resignation and, after making a "long detailed examination of his conscience,"[74] write a memorandum of defense. Of course the resignation is taken by everyone as virtually an admission of guilt.

Just before Vanaan leaves, Elena, his teen-age daughter, arrives. When she enters an *"harmonious sound, as of a bugle"*[75] can be heard twice. She comes to pick up her father. When they are about to leave, Cust sees her and is struck by her. Betti presents Elena as the symbol of innocence in the world and in every man. The harmonious sound which accompanies her entrance is a faraway echo of the lost innocence Cust has almost forgotten he once possessed. Besides the bugle's sound, there is another detail to guide the spectator in perceiving Elena as a symbol: although Vanaan has been working there for years, this is the first time she has come into the building. The playwright needed at this point in the play some device, some image to exteriorize theatrically a pivotal moment that gives a new direction to the investigation and to the drama itself.

Whether Elena is to be interpreted at this point as Grace, as a Freudian *via regia*, or as a Jungian paychompomp is not important to experiencing the journey. Theatrically she is the age-old device of the *deus ex machina*. She comes into the building for the first time in her and in Cust's lifetime, and she induces in him an epiphanic moment. After she and her father leave, her image forces Cust to investigate his own life for the first time, which now appears to him in a sinister light. Elena's image slowly pushes him backward in time: at first Elena is his daughter, then she becomes his wife, and then, further back still, she is transformed into his innocent mother, and he into a pure child. This ghost of an unlived life guided by innocence makes him more keenly aware of his life. He exclaims: "My God, how horrible the whole thing is. What a wasted life."[76] At the end of Act I, Erzi hints that perhaps the investigation is over, but Cust, in his subconscious desire to be caught and to atone, suggests that he continue.

In Act II Cust pretends to help in the inquiry. Croz, the most cynical of the judges, suspects him, but Cust is too cunning for them. In the middle of the act, Elena brings the memorandum Vanaan wrote, which will clear him of every suspicion and will point to the real culprit. Cust is the only one present; he pretends to be the investigator and takes the memorandum. They confront each other, innocence and corruption. Elena defends her father. What Cust really would like to do is confess his guilt to her and his attraction for her innocence. But since Elena in her pride cannot admit that the smallest blemish touches her father, Cust (himself blemished) feels rejected and his love turns to hate. He tells her of Vanaan's shadowy side; that he is as corrupt as every other human being; that only the young are innocent and as pure as crystal. Even Elena—he insists—will lose her innocence, just as he did when as a child he saw his parents mating. Until then he had not really known them or himself. Elena, horrified, is now convinced of her father's guilt. She runs away and throws herself down an elevator shaft.

During her fall she screams, but Cust, who is on stage with Erzi and Croz, is the only one to hear her. When she is carried in, he is terrified and pleads: "Elena, don't die."[77] He sees blood on his hand and, cleaning it hysterically, says: "I haven't touched her."[78] When at the end of the act Vanaan arrives, Cust screams at him what he wants to say to himself: "You will never be in peace! (*Raising his voice*) Nevermore, nevermore in peace,

Vanaan."[79] The hysterical rubbing of the hand and these last lines of course remind us of Lady Macbeth.

Cust has reached the nadir of his corruption. He has tried to kill even the remembrance of his lost innocence. He is alone and desperate. His only desire, not consciously admitted, is to confess. In Act III, still haunted by his bloody hand, he says to Croz: "Look at this hand; I have to make an effort to keep myself from cleaning it, while it is already perfectly clean."[80] Croz fakes a heart attack, and Cust, believing Croz is dying, confesses: "Yes, Croz, I was the man we all looked for. I really needed, needed, to tell somebody. I couldn't stand it any longer."[81] Croz, who really is near death, still has enough strength to make Cust's confession public, but he does not. He doesn't believe in duty or human justice. For him "things develop...according to purely vegetable laws."[82] He is one of the most cynical characters in Betti's theater: he cannot understand why something is right and another wrong, since "the main hook is missing, the original hook."[83] Judge Parsc, in *Landslide*, also cannot find a "fixed point,"[84] but Parsc is tormented. Croz cannot conceive of the possibility of a law governing human existence. If Elena represents in regard to Cust the *terminus ad quem*, Croz is the *terminus a quo*, devoid of any spark of desire for salvation; his torment is physical, the pain in his moribund body. He understands Cust's torment and his longing for confession, but, in a final defiance of man's ideals, he accuses himself before he dies instead of revealing Cust's secret and liberating him.

Once again, as at the end of the first and the second act, Cust remains free and undetected. In the first act he had blamed Vanaan; in the second he had destroyed the accusatory memorandum; at the end of the play, in an ironic twist, in spite of his confession and his willingness to be caught, he is about to receive the nomination to the Council Presidency. Everyone congratulates him. Vanaan, now cleared, also arrives; he has become feeble and senile; he thinks Elena died many years ago as a child. He says: "I hope for Paradise, and I don't want to know anything else."[85] He exits for the last time with the line: "[God] is good. He forgives. He forgets. And we too forget in his bliss."[86]

Finally Cust is officially nominated. Erzi, who seems to

suspect something, congratulates him and leaves, saying: "Let the world go on. This is being human."[87] But when Cust is about to leave, the harmonious sound of Elena's entrance is heard. He stops and since "no argument in the world could make *him* sleep peacefully tonight...[he] will confess the truth to the Alto Revisore [The Supreme Judge]."[88] He will go to him alone—he refuses the Archivist's offer to accompany him—because, as he says in the last line of the play: "I am a little scared. But I know nobody can help me."[89] He opens the door to go to the Alto Revisore, and a long staircase is revealed as the harmonious sound is heard again.

Among the six corrupted judges, the only one saved is the most corrupt and the most tormented. Cust is saved solely by his courage in looking into the abyss of his soul and in discovering himself in all his abjection. One must not make the mistake of attributing to Cust Betti's Catholic belief and faith. Betti the artist refused to do so. Cust's tragedy lies in the despair of self-knowledge, in his struggle with his destiny of corruption. Betti helps the audience in avoiding this mistake by having the play's only orthodox religious words uttered by the senile Vanaan. In *Corruption in the Palace of Justice* the accent is on hellish self-torment not purgatorial atonement or paradisiacal bliss. But from the moment he realizes he is lost in the dark wood, man's journey on the right path can start.

VI. The Inquiry

It is pertinent to think with Ottavio Spadaro[90] that *Ispezione* (1945–1946; *The Inquiry*, 1966), could be the title not just of one but of all Betti's plays. In almost all of them the purpose of the story is to discover something: official inquiries in *Landslide*, *Corruption in the Palace of Justice* and *Irene innocente* try to uncover facts; unofficial ones in *The House on the Water*, *Night in the Rich Man's House*, and *Goat Island*, represent metaphysical quests. Both types, though, are attempts to strip away those layers—psychoses, lies, myths, beliefs, avowed feelings, ideals—around the truth of man's condition which make that condition more bearable or at least less unbearable.

Nevertheless, *The Inquiry* is unique. It is an official inquiry, but after a while by a strange turn it becomes a probing into the private lives of the characters and then into human lives in general. At the start the Inspector presents himself as an official member of the police department; later he reveals himself as someone who knew the characters many years before; finally he becomes a kind of ultimate judge from whom it is impossible to hide the truth.

In the notes he wrote while drafting the play Betti mentions that the Inspector was born "with difficulty," and that he (Betti) was not sure if he should be a "realistic or a metaphysical figure."[91] In fact, Betti preferred to change the Inspector during the play from quasi-realistic to quasi-metaphysical. It is the change that differentiates him from the two other official inquirers we have already met, Goetz of *Landslide* and Erzi of *Corruption in the Palace of Justice*—even if, as Di Pietro observes, he is as "ambiguous and allusive"[92] as they are. He is from the start a "Kafkaesque"[93] inspector, insensitive, insinuating, mocking, sarcastic, cruel, and psychologically unrealistic. The changes he goes through are not arbitrary but gradual, and they parallel the play itself. The Inspector changes in that the more the other characters reveal themselves, the more powerful he has to become in order to probe further.

If the Inspector is ambiguous and not believable, the inquiry itself appears even less believable. In the three other plays of official inquiry there is something definite to be investigated: Who is responsible for the cave-in at the railroad? Which judge was bribed to reveal the secret decision of the Council? Are Irene and her family guilty of corrupting the morals of the village? In *The Inquiry* it is never stated exactly what, why, or even who is being investigated. Actually, as the play unfolds there are three kinds of investigation, a different one for each act. And while in the other three plays something has happened before the play starts to warrant the investigation (which the audience is informed of right at the beginning) in *The Inquiry* nothing specific has happened or at least what has happened remains unmentioned, just as this Inspector remains nameless.

Another aspect which differentiates this drama from the

other three trial-plays is that whereas the plots of *Landslide* and *Irene innocente* involve a whole town, and *Corruption in the Palace of Justice* concentrates mainly on one individual, the plot of *The Inquiry* concerns a family.

Although it may be true that this play lacks a "real and proper narrative movement, and a succession of facts" which G.M. Guglielmino believes "really necessary in a theatrical piece,"[94] we cannot agree with Moro's remark about the "absence of life and action in the characters."[95] Perhaps there is no action but certainly there is passion: in this drama one finds more "pleasure in words than in action,"[96] and this lack of action makes successful performance difficult. Still, some critics argue (and we concur that *The Inquiry* is "among the best"[97] by Betti.

At the raising of the curtain a tableau greets us. "*The meal has just ended.... [It] is that time of laziness just after a heavy lunch*"[98]: an old lady, Egle; a young woman, her daughter Iole; Iole's fiancé, Ferdinando; Engle's other daughter, forty-year-old Emma; Emma's husband, Andrea; and their child, Giulio; are still sitting around the table. The torpor emanating from their satiated bodies suggests how physical instinct is the mainspring of their relationships. They are on "the bottom rung of the ladder" Betti believed they would strive to ascend. Only, these characters won't ascend. This drama represents the "destruction"[99] of their every myth; "one of the cruellest plays which appeared in Italy after World War II,"[100] Silvio D'Amico wrote in 1955. Its first critics in 1947, who "underlined...[its] negative, cynical and disgusting attitude,"[101] mistook the stage for their neighborhoods. (One can doubt whether life has meaning but not whether theater has.)

Betti certainly was aware of the cruel and crude elements of *The Inquiry*. The first thing that happens on stage is that the child, Giulio, runs out and will not come back again. Without his presence the other members of the family, and Betti too, will feel freer to talk of sordid details. It must be noted that the duration of the story is about three hours and that the other characters could have spoken about Giulio without the audience thinking his complete absence from the stage strange. (He is mentioned once not out of love, but hate.) Betti "planned" his momentary presence and swift exit. The child leaves and so does the innocence he typically symbolizes in Betti.

The adults who remain on stage have been war refugees for two years, and now they are staying in a boardinghouse. The two daughters, the husband, and the fiancé think the old and sickly Egle is hiding the family money her husband left. They hate her for it. She is aware of it, she even thinks they would like to kill her, and as if to challenge and torture them she leaves her poisonous medicine right on top of the bureau in the dining room in a place where anyone can take it. She is friendly only with the young handyman Zeffirino; in this she reminds us of Federica in *Spiritism in the Ancient House*. Zeffirino helps her walk; they play cards together, and at times they play at being children. Now, after lunch, they leave together.

The other four lazily make plans to go to the last movie show, and then the doorbell rings. And before the landlady goes to answer it, to our surprise *"although no one has opened the door, two men have entered."*[102] This entrance is the first sign of the unreal aspect of the Inspector; of the two men only he will speak throughout the play. We notice another sign of his strangeness in scene ii when he remains alone with the landlady. She says in reference to the others: "They are a family," and the Inspector in a most unexpected and illogical way responds: "What do you mean by that?"[103] This is an important question, the first one of the inquiry, and from it we can already surmise that it will be an inquiry out of the ordinary, the most extraordinary of all Betti's official inquiries. It puts into question and doubt the meaning of even the commonest and most ordinary statement. By the end of the play the spectator will still not exactly know why the Inspector came. Achille Fiocco writes that he "perhaps came on his own, perhaps called forth by a thousand undefinable desires."[104]

Once the inquiry begins, the juxtaposition of the inquisitor and the displaced family creates an opposition among the members of the family itself. In Act I, scene iii, Andrea asks: "Can you tell me what the purpose of this inquiry is?" The Inspector answers in a Beckett-like fashion: "Actually, we've been sent by the authorities. We carry out orders. We're here for information."[105] He vaguely tells him that maybe one of them sent

an appeal complaining about something. When Andrea, Ferdinando, Emma, and Iole are together with the Inspector, they
don't voice any complaint except that they wish to be home
again. Andrea says: "I'm waiting for someone to decide to repatriate us,"[106] and Ferdinando: "We all want to go home."[107]
But, if together they act as a displaced family anxious to be re-
stored to the normalcy of their lives, when they individually face
the Inspector, each reveals a suspicion of the others. Ferdinando,
who is the first to be alone with the Inspector, states: "Maybe
they said something nasty about me."[108] Even the handyman,
Egle's friend, asks: "What did they tell you?"[109] When it is
Emma's turn, she also appears suspicious: "Has my husband told
you something?"[110] Iole: "I'm sure they've already told you about
me."[111] Then Andrea: "There is a person here who...would be
very glad to hurt me. I think [he] has already spoken to you about
me."[112] Finally, the old lady: "Did they call you for me?"[113]
These obsessions keep the spectator's interest throughout the first
act; he is waiting for the revelation of some crime about which
the Inspector must already know. But as the scenes follow and
the rhythmic crescendo of the *leitmotif* of the suspicion encom-
passes everyone on stage with the relentless theatricality of two-
player scenes, the effect is of a nightmare.

Betti has succeeded in sublimating the particular fear of each
into an anxiety of the unknown. At a certain point what we, as
spectators, ask is not why each is afraid but why he shouldn't be.
The helplessness and vulnerability of the characters is given a
factual base in their condition as exiles. At first the uneasiness of
all (except Egle) seems to be the result of being in a strange place.
Andrea: "If you're here about the repatriation, I can assure you
we're absolutely entitled to it."[114] His wife, Emma: "We have a
right to it, our repatriation,"[115] And Ferdinando, speaking for
everybody: "But living here is a real drag. We all want to go
home."[116]

However, when each of them alone confronts the Inspector,
his words reveal a preoccupation which is not just caused by the
strange place in which he lives. Ferdinando explains: "We've been
thrust outside, without anything: no cocoon, nothing." Then he
adds the most penetrating line of the first act: "Naked. We have

to be what we really are."[117] The whole play can be considered an explanation of this line, which will become monstrously clear by the end of the drama. Emma confesses that the fault is hers and that "what it amounts to is that I'm just no longer young"[118] — that's why she thinks everyone hates her. Iole informs the Inspector crudely: "I think the family is the place where the most ridiculous and least respectable things in the world go on."[119] Andrea, after speaking vividly of menstrual blood, sweat, dirty underwear, of the "real smell of life without euphemism," concludes that "Perhaps the reason is this: that even when things go well, they're still going poorly. If for no other reason, because we grow old."[120]

At the end of the act, while Andrea is still talking, Egle enters. She and Andrea fight over the money she doesn't want to share with her daughters, who now are watching from the door. Her son-in-law, feeling humiliated, turns to the Inspector and begins to tell how successful he was as a student, how he "was a big man." The Inspector surprisingly, matter of factly, *"quietly"* informs them, only now, that he is a fellow-citizen and that he knew them all twenty years ago. He remembers how people were attracted by Andrea's conversation at the Gallery Café; how beautiful Emma was then; how cute Iole looked walking with her parents "in a little dress of tulle." They all are shocked at the Inspector's revelation, and feel as if they are spied on. Andrea tells him they wouldn't have spoken of their personal lives to someone who knew them. Only the Inspector and Egle remain on the stage; he remembers how lovely and happy Egle looked. She objects that she was never happy, she was just living a stupid daily routine. She too is mad at him and asks if he is a real inspector and who called him. As the act ends, he replies *"slowly pointing his finger at her*: 'You.'"[121]

Act II begins with the same scene without a lapse of time. But instead of finally finding out the purpose of the inquiry, we are told that indeed Egle had written to the police, but many years before, and as a mother beside herself at the death of her little son. Enraged, she wanted to accuse the doctor of negligence. But now Egle doesn't remember the boy's name, and doesn't want to ask anyone for fear of being thought senile. This is surely the only instance in literature of a mother not mentally ill who doesn't remember her dead son's name.

We learned at first that the family is uncomfortable with someone from their past, then that Egle has cancelled the dearest memory of that past. Exile is not only geographic (in space) but also historical (in time). Betti has prepared the spectator for a new kind of inquiry. The Inspector now chooses to reveal the purpose of his visit—to tell them news of their repatriation. Nevertheless, the Inspector continues to question them. In the first scene of Act II he tells Egle: "The truth. It's not always easy. We go deeper and deeper, but we never find it. Up to now you have all been reticent."[122]

The reason the inquiry goes on, must go on, apparently is because the two couples don't actually want to be repatriated. In Act I, they had all expressed the desire to go back to their former lives and homes. Now they complain not of the burden of their lives as refugees, but of the misery of their lives per se. Before, they were saying, We are unhappy here; now they say, We are unhappy with ourselves. For Andrea the only important question, despite his success in being a good lawyer and in having a family, is: "But for me? What about myself?"[123] He feels that in his life "nothing has happened."[124] He wishes for "something that will... let us say: 'Yes. There it is. Now we've made it. This was worth my while. This I'll remember.'"[125] These last words are overheard by Egle who mocks him by telling the Inspector her son-in-law "makes speeches. He'll always use big words."[126] This conflict reminds us of the most famous family in Italian theater, the six characters in search of an author. Among them the Son accuses the Father of hiding behind "phrases, phrases" and "literature, literature!" The Stepdaughter accuses him of inventing "intellectual complications."[127] As in the *Six Characters in Search of an Author*, this second act of *The Inquiry* will also unveil a tale of sordid sexuality, shame, and degradation. The spectator gets a first hint of it when Egle, in the third scene, explains to the Inspector: "He [Andrea] is always emitting grand statements.... But all there is underneath is something cheap and dirty."[128]

When Andrea decides: "I just don't want to go back home,"[129] it changes not only everyone's attitude, but also the structure of the play. In the first act each member had a revelatory moment *a solo* with the Inspector; now what is revealed comes from the interchange among family members. In Act I, with the pretense of escape through repatriation, they could also pretend that they possessed individual freedom; now that that pretense is shattered, they have to expose their feelings, condemned, as they are, in the cage of their senses.

It is a degrading *ménage à quatre*. Andrea's and Emma's marriage has been a "mistake, from first to last, a great mistake, but no one's fault."[130] Betti seems to have founded this family on hate: they fight about their son, to whom Emma feels "chained,"[131] for Giulio would remain with her after her separation from Andrea, who is having an affair with Iole. But this relation is also devoid of love. According to Iole it started because: "I realized he didn't know what to do with his life...[and] I didn't know what to do with mine either. So I went to him."[132] Ferdinando, her fiancé, has always known about it and thinks of Andrea as a "poor dope" since "He's the one who is in the dark."[133] The two sisters also hate each other, and their mother; Egle, who hates Andrea and even rejects Zeffirino, her play-partner, sums it up: "They're all against me. And the reason is that I'm the mother.... Everything comes from me. Without me they'd be nothing. And they blame me for that."[134] They suffer just because they were born, and they have no escape, as Egle implies: "But you'll obey me, my dears. Because you must."[135] They have no use for repatriation.

One question remains dangling throughout Act II: Why has the inquiry continued if the Inspector's task (to bring permission to repatriate) has been accomplished? Why would he continue to stay and question, and, more curiously, why would the others allow his incessant questioning into their intimate lives? In any case the questioner in Act II is no longer an inspector. Betti changed him into a judge, and the dining room into a tribunal. The Inspector says in scene iv: "This is a court of justice."[136] The others act as if they were in a tribunal; at the act's end Ferdinando addresses the Inspector as if he were a judge delivering a verdict: "What does the judge think?.... Well now, what measure are you going to take?"[137]

When the second act ends Andrea and Iole will perhaps continue their degrading relationship. But the other ties — paternal, maternal, fraternal, filial, marital — are broken. It doesn't seem that much could be added, except murder or suicide in the tradition of classical and Elizabethan tragedy. For it appears that someone has killed Egle since the poison has been stolen from the bureau.

In the first scene of Act III, everyone gathers around the Inspector who speaks as a judge: "you now stand before justice.... The guilty person...or persons...whatever the crime, will be discovered and punished."[138] But soon Betti introduces another change: the Inspector is not just a judge. He is not only interested in the crime but in conscience; he wants now to unveil guilty desires. When Emma, believing Egle poisoned, hysterically shouts: "It wasn't me!" he answers: "But you wanted it to happen," and "You've already committed the crime, many times, in your secret thoughts."[139]

Emma is also the first to confess — she doesn't really want her husband back; thinking he was the one killed, she felt great relief. Iole too confesses — she doesn't wish to go away with Andrea; she has always "despised him, hated him."[140] If she had stolen the poison, she would have used it on herself or on Andrea. Andrea has also lied — he didn't really want to live with Iole; he also wished somebody had killed Emma, Iole, Ferdinando, or all of them. He, in fact, has stolen the poison without having decided what to do with it, whom to kill; he was ready to kill anybody, including himself. In this twentieth century tragedy, suicide and murder take place in the psyche not on the stage.

Andrea feels "entangled in something without wanting to be,"[141] and he hopes for a "breakthrough, a miracle...to get control of things."[142] This is why he took the poison. He confesses that Egle was right, he has been faking. Like everyone else, he uses "empty words...[with] a theatrical ring in his voice."[143] Nor has he used the poison: Egle died a normal death, of old age. But at the end of the play, in another typically Bettian scene, her ghost appears, and, from the distance of infinity, seems to say the last word: people fake not only when they say they love but also when they say they hate. The truth is that "we don't care at all."[144]

The others would like some word of hope, and Andrea turns to the Inspector and asks him to "at least say something."[145] But the Inspector, before exiting, merely retorts: "Each one of you alone.... Alone! Rest assured of this: no one will help you."[146]

The play ends with the horror of normal life and normal death. "Everything goes back to normal."[147] The couples will do what they were planning a few hours before—they will go to the movies, where, alone in the dark, they will pretend to be together.

Who is the Inspector? He functions as a catalyst who forces the characters to look at themselves, to search and discover who they really are. In Act I, scene vii, he says: "A day comes when you have to close your eyes and be sincere."[148] He will urge them continuously toward the truth (*e.g.*: I, viii; II, i; *Ibid.*; II, ii; III, i).[149] Andrea says to him: "It is your being here that made me think."[150] And later: "It's your fault. You're the one who started talking...about balances. And now you've got to listen to us."[151] One critic thinks that his "function is finally pleonastic."[152] It would be possible to conceive of the characters in their search without the Inspector, if we consider him as their conscience. He is part of them, and that he is nameless making it easier to accept this view. Furthermore, he cannot be kept out—he enters without anybody opening the door for him—and he is, just like conscience, always present. He participates in every scene.

We should also consider the meaning of the end of the play. Andrea, before exiting, *"suddenly seized by a kind of despair,... covers his face with his hand"*[153] and remembers the vanished dreams of his youth. One critic interprets the scene as a "stimulus to purification and redemption."[154] But to impose on the play a less than dark view is to distort it. Silvio D'Amico writes that the drama concludes with "a return to its atrocious starting point," and J.A. Scott who is of the opinion (wrong, we think) that Betti "does portray a fundamentally optimistic vision of life,"[156] writes: "*Ispezione* is, however, an exception in Betti's work, for it ends with a completely negative answer."[157] We believe that *The Inquiry* ends neither with the pity and shared suffering of *Landslide* nor with the redemptive glimpse of *Corruption in the Palace of Justice*. Andrea and the others will live and die normally, in silent anguish and meaninglessness. At the beginning of the play the landlady tells the Inspector, "They are a family." We too can respond at the end with the Inspector's question: "What do you mean by that?"

VII. Crime on Goat Island

In *The Inquiry* Andrea, whom everyone suspects of having poisoned his mother-in-law, recounts a story he once heard of a mother and two daughters living in an isolated house. A stranger came and possessed all three, but one day fell into a well; the women left him there to die. As many critics have pointed out, this story is the plot of *Delitto all'Isola delle Capre* (1946; *Crime on Goat Island*, 1961[158]), save that now one of the daughters is a sister-in-law. Not pointed out is another, more important, connection between the two plays: Andrea, while still having a sexual relation with his wife, is having an affair with her sister, and both women know.

Sexual references, direct or indirect, are frequent in many of Betti's plays and recur throughout his career. From a moralistic stand, they may appear crude, lecherous, or in violation of a tabu like incest in *Troubled Waters*. In regard to *Goat Island* (1966)[159] Di Pietro, the only critic to inspect Betti's notebooks, informs us of "an allusion to a man who, arriving at a house inhabited only by women, makes them fall in love with him"[160] as well as of other, less specific, allusions "that have only vague analogies to the story of *Goat Island*."[161] But what is interesting is not their relation to the play, for the fact that they are *not* directly related to *Goat Island* renders them more revealing and important in regard to the author in general. They are another sign that Betti is not just obsessed with the quest for justice but also with the analysis of sexual relations outside accepted morality and mores.

We agree, however, with G.H. McWilliam that Betti's "pre-occupation with sexual matters should not be mistaken for a narrow puritanism. He shows no desire to preach.... On the contrary Betti accepts the libidinous impulse as a natural and inalterable element in man."[162] Several plays like *Landslide* or

Corruption in the Palace of Justice are concerned mainly with the quest for justice; others, like *The Inquiry* and *Irene innocente*, combine an interest in justice with unethical sexual relations; still others like *An Inn on the Harbor, Goat Island, Struggle Till Dawn,* or *Troubled Waters* are mainly concerned with tabu sexuality, although these last ones also take the form of a kind of inquest. Whether the play is apparently about justice or sex, the playwright's poetic is the traditional quest of what a man is.

Why these two obesssions and not others? We have written above that the investigative method with which Betti constructs his plays is the expression of a religious artist who is obsessed by the lack of an explanation for the presence of evil in man. Nor is it surprising that for a Christian believer like Betti evil is in part symbolized in the most traditionally inculcated way: as a sin of the flesh. We are not making a statement about Betti the individual; a psychoanalytical study of his work, and especially of his extensive notes, has not been conducted, though such a study would certainly reveal some interesting aspects of his personality.

Obviously it is not the sin per se Betti was interested in but the sin *qua* metaphor. Of the two abysses which can rob a man of his humanity—becoming machine-like (modern and Marxian) or regressing to an animal-like status (classical and Hegelian)—Betti feared the second. For Betti man lives in a tension between Circe's call of unconscious instinctuality (sensuality) and the call of self-awareness (spirituality).

Usually the struggle in Betti's plays is to reach the life of the spirit, to break out of the prison of finitude. The exceptions are *The Inquiry* and *Goat Island.* In fact, it seems that their compositions overlap. In the first, the characters will remain damned in the pain of living together but will maintain a pretense of the human and the "normal." They also will have no exit. *Goat Island* is unique in that it destroys even that pretense and portrays man in his finite animality.

There are two statements, one in each play, which link them, and which indiciate that they originated from a similar spark, at a similar moment of inspiration. In the fifth scene of Act I in *The Inquiry* Ferdinando tells the Inspector: "No cocoon, nothing. Naked. We have to be what we really are."[163] He means that without the defenses of civilization they are powerless to resist the drowning wave of the unexamined life—that examination which is the basis of Western civilization.

Echoing Ferdinando's words, Agata says: "The important thing is to understand what we are, and to be it; and then everything becomes simple...[one can] rest: like the grass, the animals, like stones. That's what I want."[164] In Agata, Betti created a new Pasiphaë. And as Angelo explains: "She became a beast and gave herself to a bull. This is not something of the senses...it is something in the soul. The soul...wants to...cure . self of being human."[165] Betti was worried during the composition of this play lest its real drama be "stifled 'in the old realistic-sexual mold.'"[166]

Again Betti faces, as most critics notice, the theme of good and evil. But what makes this play special is that Betti is now focusing on the struggle of to be or not to be a man, in the sense of "obeying" the instinctual flesh or striving for spiritual values. *Goat Island* is a religious drama because, as H.D.F. Kitto says in another context, "the real focus lies not in one or more characters, but somewhere behind them."[167] Behind "the Tragic Hero...is the divine background."[168] It is not that the drama necessarily presupposes Betti's Catholic theology. What is awe-provoking is the possibility which accompanies man all his life, of being drawn back to the origin of human history, of losing any trace of individuality, of living through impulses instead of ideals. In this play Betti confronts his audience with the Socratic question, πῶς δεῖ ζῆν, how shall we live our life?

Unlike most of Betti's plays, the story of *Goat Island* doesn't directly present a struggle. Right at the start, the main characters are already what they will be at the end of the play; there will be neither *askesis* nor *descensus*. But the spectator will be asking himself again or for the first time, πῶς δεῖ ζῆν. For the answer to the question will characterize the deeds and existence of one's life and will give the individual his essence. As Agata says: "There is a point at which we choose what we are."[169] At that point she feels that her true life is in the senses. When the angel appears to her to announce: "Our salvation lies in sin,"[170] she has already made the decision by herself.

Like Betti's other strangers or investigators who cause an

upheaval in the main characters—whose disturbing presence provokes those characters to acts of discovery about themselves or about the unbearability of their surrounding—the foreigner Angelo awakens Agata and forces her to face her decision. Angelo is a metaphorical exteriorization of the stranger within Agata—within us all. He is the one who will seduce Pia and Silvia, but before he comes, Agata has tried to seduce them herself by compelling them to live on Goat Island, an unnatural island because it is grassy land in the middle of a desert, not in the sea. Agata is keeping them here in the constant presence of goats, ancient symbols of lechery. She finds such surroundings most natural, and this is the first relevant fact that we, with the "inspector" Angelo, discover. The second is that Agata brought also her husband here from the city. He was her opposite: he believed and tried to live according to higher principles and for a time she herself wanted to believe them. What prevented her was the fact that her husband had human failings also, and was compromised by his senses. Agata was too proud to compromise; she confesses that what happened was "because of *her* pride"[171]; she wanted "either everything or nothing."[172] She thought that her husband was "deceiving *her*...making *her* believe things he himself didn't really believe."[173] So she chose the other path, and he abandoned her rather than succumb to her. Nevertheless, we learn that he too, near the end of his life, was seduced by Agata's memory. As Angelo recounts it, he remembered and desired Agata only as she was at night, during their moments of passion.

Since it is she who is the seducer in the play, and Angelo, in a sense, her own inner self, Betti, an experienced and deft playwright, presents the attraction they feel for one another right at their first meeting, as if it were predestined. This is also why Agata is so sure Angelo will come back, though she has sent him away, and also why Angelo is so sure he can come back and find the door open.

The despair of the first act—the monotonous visitations of Eduardo's truck, the continuous slamming of the broken shutter by the night wind, the incessant bleating of the goats, the island in the middle of a hot and dry desert—culminates as Agata in the dark opens the door and lies down on a pile of goatskins to wait for Angelo. Judged by psychologically realistic standards Act I doesn't convey much signification, but Betti has organized and controlled the building blocks in such a way that its ending not only appears believable but is charged with the meaning of the whole play. Agata here is giving one possible answer to the Socratic question: she opens the door of her house, she lowers her body to the earth as far away from heaven as possible, and with the smell of animals in her nostrils spreads herself — and this is the true way to act out the scene — in order to accept the domination of her god. We have to react not to a naturalistic scene but to a scene from the symbolic theater.

At the end of Act I, suspense has overtaken the spectator: Is he also tempted by Agata? Was he seduced by the apparently sweet voice of renunciation? — Angelo had said: "I'm lucky, I can sleep at night."[174] Was he desiring to substitute himself for Angelo and join Agata on the goatskins? If he says yes, even for a second, Agata has won.

When Act II opens, Angelo has already seduced Agata's sister-in-law, Pia, and Agata's daughter, Silvia. Pia was willing despite her dream of living in contact with art and beauty, as she had done years ago in Vienna; Silvia couldn't resist and her innocence was brutally trampled upon. Agata, aware of everything, silently acquiesces, and all three feel they have to "obey" Angelo. Why? When Agata accepted him, she did it not only for herself and not only for all the household — she opened the door of the house — she accepted him for all humanity. By this we do not only mean that Agata may be seen as the symbol of fallen humanity — though she is that too. In fact, one cannot solve a metaphysical question and suppose the solution is valid only for oneself. When in Act II, scene iii, she is confronted by Silvia, Agata wants to avoid any discussion of Angelo and the three women. Later, in the fifth scene, when Silvia screams at her: "Mother, I'm already lost,"[175] Agata answers: "When you were small...I was so full of compassion for you."[176] Her reaction seems to mean: "I cannot have compassion for you now."

Silvia, the youngest and most innocent of the three, fights against Agata and Angelo. Although fallen, she cannot share their answer to the Socratic question — her own answer is in the name of a higher humanity, a humanity closer to angels than animals. She tells her mother: "You have agreed to renounce your humanity!"[177] Toward the end of the scene Silvia *"kneels and embraces her mother's knees,"*[178] begging her to leave the house, to renounce her life and to go away with her; Agata just runs out. A life of instincts doesn't allow reflection and contemplation: Agata still does not and cannot face all the consequences of her decision, which, once taken, is valid for all humanity. She cannot admit innocence into her world view.

The next time Agata sees her, Silvia will be on the floor almost prostrate before Angelo, after trying to shoot him. While Angelo speaks, she interrupts him three times saying: "I want to die."[179] This is the pivotal point of the play, in which the world of the spirit is vanquished. The spectator, who for a split second was attracted by Agata, has run the risk of dying in his soul—the same risk Dante remembers when he meets Paolo and Francesca in Hell and, realizing how close he has come to the abyss, faints out of terror.

At the end of the second act the three women are willing to live a goatish life with Angelo as their shepherd. To celebrate his victory he climbs down a well to fetch some bottles; the rope ladder breaks and, unless Agata throws him a rope, he cannot climb up. It is not the well of life but of death the audience is presented with. Again Agata has to decide.

Act III starts two days and two nights later: Angelo is still in the well. Agata sends Pia and Silvia away from Goat Island, telling them that she will then let Angelo come up. She can't, we mean, allow the contamination of the whole world. Angelo's call has now become a "howling," but still Agata doesn't respond. She knows she cannot be saved and, in fact, agrees with Angelo's judgment: "poor Agata. You will be condemned and cursed for all eternity."[180] She answers: "But that's exactly what gives me peace. To receive what I deserve."[181] While *Corruption in the Palace of Justice* ended with the hope of redemption, *Landslide* with a brotherhood of suffering and guilt, *The Inquiry* with the horror of desperate normality, *Goat Island* ends for the main character with eternal anguish. But this anguish, in spite of Betti's Catholicism, is not caused by a superior being. Agata is not Eve who displeased God and was exiled. It is not necessary for the spectator to postulate a Catholic metaphysic in order to lend meaning to Agata's circumstances. Hers is self-willed suffering. She is one of Betti's more convincing existential characters. She is aware of having chosen her path herself, and she believes that whatever comes of her choice has to become her own self. She had already said in the first act: "Rather than chaos or nothing after death, I prefer to think of punishment."[182] Now, at the end of the play, she doesn't reject her existence. For she has created it and in so doing she has created herself. She says: "I love my burden.... There is a point at which we choose what we are.... In the end there is always a certain peace in being what one is, in being that completely."[183]

Her only wish is to save her daughter. For Silvia has not chosen but was "dragged into this."[184] Agata has to cut "a kind of root between *them* and the earth, a kind of gut...[an] umbilicus"[185] with which Angelo pulls them.

After Pia and Silvia leave, Agata rushes to the well, lowers a rope and entreats Angelo to come up, but he is already dead. She hoped he was still alive, but from this hope the spectator shouldn't think that she wanted to play a trick on the other two women. Such a trick would force the play into "the old realistic-sexual mold"[186] Betti wants to avoid. Agata meant to leave Angelo in the well as long as Pia and Silvia remained in the house, no matter how long it took. Her decision was firm, and that is why Act III starts with Agata brooding, while Angelo is down the well, about "the concept of eternity."[187] We cannot agree with the critic who argues: "She [Agata] is guided by an indecision [whether to pull Angelo out or not] prolonged to such a point that it becomes decision."[188]

It is important that the cause of her doom is her decision and not the effect of circumstance. For beside being a religious tragedy in the sense H.D.F. Kitto understands it, *Goat Island* is a Christian tragedy in Auden's sense, a "tragedy of possibility."[189] In fact, we can say of Agata Auden's words in another context: "What a pity it was this way when it might have been otherwise."[190] This other possibility remains open for Pia, Silvia, and the spectator.

Angelo's death is one crime on Goat Island. Agata now

closes the door and windows and in the dark speaks the play's last line to dead Angelo: "We'll simply go on calling out to each other...and fighting each other...for all eternity."[191] She will wait for her own death in the dark, or maybe she will throw herself into the well—just as Silvia, a few minutes before, still under Angelo's spell, threatened to do. Agata's prospective suicide is another crime on the island. A third is the metaphysical crime of attempting to kill the loftier aspirations of humanity.

Although it was "chosen by the judges of a *Concorso Nazionale*"[192] to be performed in the year of its composition, 1946, *Goat Island* was not, in fact, first performed until 20 October 1950, in Rome. It was a fiasco. Eight days later the performance was repeated in Milan where it also failed. Among other things Betti was accused of an improper interest in "sexual pathology,"[193] and of a "turbid, lewd, and restless imagination."[194] Three years later, on 23 April 1953, the play had its foreign première in Paris, and it became a clamorous theatrical success with critics and public. It ran for almost a year, and Betti acquired an international reputation. In 1954, the play was performed in Belgium, Germany, Spain, and the United States. It has since been performed around the world.[195]

After the French triumph, Betti was acclaimed Italy's most important playwright after Pirandello. Yet in 1973, in Italy, one critic still tried to diminish this triumph by attributing it to a "laical not religious" interpretation of the play.[196] *Goat Island* suffered the same vicissitudes as *Six Characters in Search of an Author*, which received catcalls in Rome, gaining international fame only after its triumph in Milan and Paris. Jean Neveux, after attending the première of Betti's play in Paris, wrote: "Exactly thirty years ago an elevator [Georges Pitoëff had used an elevator at the rear of the stage for summoning the six characters] came down the stage of the *Champs-Elysées* theater and placed there six unexpected characters dreamed up by Luigi Pirandello.... The evening of the first presentation of *Goat Island* I had a similarly unusual impression: the impression that a new theater once again was about to materialize before our eyes."[197] Whether or not Betti's play has the same importance for the evolution of theater as Pirandello's, it will remain important.

Chapter 5

In Search of Meaning

> *Impossibility is a stone wall.... I mean to say, a*
> *wall is a wall.... Naturally I shan't break through*
> *the wall with my head, if I'm really not strong*
> *enough, but I won't be reconciled to it simply*
> *because it's a stone wall and I haven't enough*
> *strength to break it down*
> (Dostoyevsky, *Notes from Underground*).

After the perplexing impasse of *Landslide* and *The Duck
Hunter*, Betti, as we have observed, wrote only comedies from
1934 to 1938, as if to forget what he could not resolve. When in
1938 he returned to his real artistic and intellectual concerns, he
attempted to resolve the old impasse. With the next five plays he
composed—*Night in the Rich Man's House*, *The Night Wind*,
Husband and Wife, *Spiritism in the Ancient House*, and *Corruption in the Palace of Justice*—he presents, however faintly and
however these plays do differ, a belief, or hope, or a desperate
challenge, which asserts that there is an order in the universe
within which the ugliness, injustice, and chaos of the human
condition will be atoned for or erased.

In *The Inquiry* and *Goat Island* the artist depicts man in the
abyss: instinctual impulses seem to dominate the individual. Each

drama concludes with the relegation and condemnation of the main characters to despair: these two plays make the student of his theater aware that Betti knew the worst. Thirteen years before—but only *qua* artist—he had avoided (what he must have felt was) an unbearable impasse. The older Betti did not side-step the searing and bleak conclusion of *The Inquiry* and *Goat Island*. In what follows he strives to discover, if not a way out, a route from desperation to hope. This struggle starts with the new play, *Lotta fino all'alba* (1947; *Struggle Till Dawn*, 1964).

I. Struggle Till Dawn

In *Struggle Till Dawn* Betti is still trapped by the dark atmosphere of his last two plays, not yet completely convinced of the possibility of salvation for his protagonist. Betti himself, in fact, thinks that *Struggle Till Dawn* is a "contradictory drama of a man who changes but actually remains himself."[1] Of course, intellectually and dramatically, there is nothing wrong with a play whose protagonist remains the same and fails to achieve the redemption he is striving for; this drama is powerful in spite of a forced ending.

The play is a "fable of sin, remorse, repentance, and beatitude,"[2] and though it is set outside the law court, it takes the form of an inquest into what happens during a man's search for authenticity and responsibility for certain actions which took place long before the drama begins. In a street accident during the war, an uncontrolled truck hit Giorgio, the protagonist. Such accidents have an important part in several of Betti's short stories and in such plays as *Landslide* and *Spiritism in the Ancient House*; they break the flow of normal events, giving rise to unexpected circumstances into whose middle some characters are thrown unprepared and "naked," forced to face themselves. After Giorgio was hit, he remained unconscious and near death for a long time; Elsa, his wife, took him away from town apparently so that he could recuperate more readily. Now, after five years, called apparently by a letter from the Notary, they have returned; before they couldn't, because of the war.

In the first scene Giorgio and Elsa are at a notary's office. The apparent reason for their six hundred mile trip is to receive compensation for lost property, but they are told by the Deputy Notary that according to the register their case is closed. After this preliminary scene, realistic and factual, a most intriguing first act follows. Giorgio insists on reliving the day of the accident, even describing its weather — "A beautiful sunny morning."[3] The Deputy Notary — and the spectator with him — is puzzled and answers: "But what does all this have to do with your claim."[4]

Alone with the Deputy Notary, Elsa explains that her husband has suffered a lot and that she wants to be "useful" to him; she doubts she acted well in taking him away from town since: "I know...that my husband probably had...different intentions."[5] When Giorgio remains alone with the Deputy Notary, he continues to speak of five years ago, his friends and acquaintances; the audience expects some kind of revelation, and so does the Deputy Notary who encourages him by saying: "Come on, tell me the truth. The notary's office is a sort of confessional."[6] But the truth is not so simple: Giorgio suggests he did something for which he is in "fear," in "terror" of being misjudged by people he hurt, if for no other reason than because he is "so different now."[7]

The Notary, on the other hand, informs Giorgio that he never sent him any letter, someone else must have; someone in town must have wanted him back. And, in fact, a man is waiting for him. Before seeing him, Giorgio realizes who he is and asks: "Is there anybody with him...a woman.... Is his wife there too?... I did him a very serious injury."[8] Waiting for him is his best friend, Tullio, whom he thought was dead. Giorgio anxiously asks him if he has discovered "anything." Tullio answers that he has not, and informs Giorgio that Delia, his wife, is dead. He mocks Giorgio, saying that surely there must have been another reason for his return, war compensation being a "feeble excuse." Giorgio admits it is so. Tullio invites his friend to his new out-of-the-way house and leaves.

The entire act is suffused with an ominous tone. More than once the spectator is brought to the brink of a fearful revelation. Giorgio is hiding something he wants to correct and be forgiven for. The Notary asks him what he wanted from him the day of the accident, for in fact Giorgio was hit a few yards from the Notary's office. Giorgio answers that he was going to the train station. The Notary observes that that was a roundabout way of going to the station.

By the end of Act I, the spectator suspects that there must have been something between Giorgio and Tullio's wife, but what is revealed in Act II is something more singular: when Giorgio was hit by the truck, he was going to the station to meet Delia and run away with her. Now he is back for...what? It is difficult for Giorgio to know. He is in such a state of crisis he is unable to discover his real feelings and why he has had to return. Most of the act is a dialogue between Giorgio and Tullio, which a critic has compared to the dialogue between Mauro and Valerio in *Night in the Rich Man's House*.[9] However, in the latter play the terms of the argument are quite clear; each determines to his own satisfaction his responsibility for action, for order or chaos in the universe, and neither of the two doubts himself. Between Giorgio and Tullio the terms of the agon are much more complex: first of all, Giorgio cannot live with the fact that a mere accident changed his life: "We cannot bear to regard ourselves simply a plaything of blind chance."[10] He is sure now he "was lying" to himself in regard to the war compensation; so he confesses "there is something in my life I wish I had never done."[11] He wants to atone for it and to forget it; he feels "trapped," and, like Mauro, Giorgio doesn't want to die "without having set everything in order."[12] He even believes in Paradise now. Tullio's intention is only to avenge himself by killing Giorgio.

In a most dramatic turn of events, Delia, who Giorgio — and the audience — was told is dead, is right there in the house. Now Giorgio is not so sure he has come back to atone. Destiny permits him to relive that fatal day, and he can decide again whether to renounce Delia or not. He is attracted by her, as he was years before; he kills Tullio, and, for the second time, they are ready to run away together. This drama, like *Goat Island*, is also a tragedy of possibility; man's destiny is within his choice.

If Betti had been possessed by the same attitude which inspired his last two dramas, this play would have concluded with the end of the second act. After years of brooding over his action, after his repentance and desire to do "anything" to correct the evil he has committed, after being convinced he is not the same person any longer, Giorgio acts in an even worse way. There is no spiritual progress for him as there was none for the protagonists in *The Inquiry* and *Goat Island*.

However, Betti's declared intention was to present "man between...goodness and evil,"[13] and Act III is a kind of medieval religious play. Elsa and Delia first fight for Giorgio, then for his soul. They are not people, they are symbols. They rehearse the last moment in a man's life: will Giorgio repent and be saved or be eternally damned? But the act is not convincing for two reasons: in the first place, Giorgio himself doesn't seem to go through the "struggle"—he appears passive. As Delia convinced him in Act II to kill Tullio, Elsa convinces him now to drink poison. The other reason is that the "struggle" between demonic Elsa and angelic Delia fails to persuade us.[14] Even if we remember, as G.H. McWilliam suggests, "that Betti is not writing in the naturalistic tradition, and that he is concerned with the dramatization of states of mind, rather than with the photographic reproduction of surface reality,"[15] Elsa and Delia still do not convince us because they are not on the same level of intensity. Delia succeeds in communicating her desperation, and she expresses the danger of living life as a "hideous mistake"; that is what will happen to Giorgio if at the end of his life he renounces what he has done. Elsa is not raised to a comparable level of goodness. At the supreme moment of saving a soul, her words sound flat and even stupid; she keeps repeating that she wants to be "useful," or "practical and dependable." One of her last incredible appeals to Giorgio is: "Please listen to the words I'll say to you. Choose the ones that are really useful, and remember them."[16] Delia's refrain, on the other hand, in the play's last moment is "Words! There's nothing else!" And "You are dying, Giorgio! And there's nothing else!" But Giorgio has already said, "Yes, Yes," to Elsa. Sergio Torresani thinks that Giorgio's suicide is a "theatrical more than a poetical necessity."[17] We can apply the same sentiment to Giorgio's conversion.

II. Irene innocente

Critics have commented that while Giorgio's salvation through suicide is not convincing, the suicide of the innocent Irene is "willed and necessary,"[18] "freely willed,"[19] and that her redemption is achieved both in the artist's intention and theatrically on stage. *Struggle Till Dawn* remains on a realistic level up to symbolic Act III, while Betti forms his next play in an unreal and symbolic mold from the beginning.

In fact, *Irene innocente* (1947) is a fable. As A. Fiocco said, commenting on this drama: "The effort of Betti's art, and its characteristic note, is to reduce reality to fable."[20] Also, because it is meant as a fable, the performance of a Roman Catholic rite which takes place at the end doesn't transform the play into a parochial pulpit. For the drama "is not moralistic; it does not preach."[21] Besides, the rite is the sacrament of matrimony which for the protagonist and her mother represents life's unreachable dream.

A suggestive scene starts the play, reminding us of the beginning of *Night in the Rich Man's House*. A traveller, Ugo, gets off a bus in a deserted place among mountains. The bus driver informs him the village he wants is two hours away, and there won't be an inn there. A second traveller, Giacomo, who also gets off the bus, recognizes Ugo from his uniform as an investigator whom the villagers expect, but he adds that "it would have been better for *him* to have stayed home."[22]

Ugo starts walking. He sings and the mountain wind brings back his singing: not an echo exactly, but "*a very far away, feminine voice*"[23] which answers his love song. Another fabulous element is the character-narrator, Nicola, who appears and tells the audience the beginning of the story: "And so he started to climb among the desert and wild mountains. He was an officer eager to advance in rank...."[24] What Nicola says will not add anything to the development of the play, but his presence introduces a distance between the play and the audience, like a Brechtian alienation effect. From now on the story is seen as a kind of allegory.

Ugo arrives at the village and knocks at the only house from whose window he can see a light, and, as in a fable, chance decrees that this be the house of the man Ugo is supposed to investigate, Augusto. The house is poor and dirty. Augusto is a humble and tattered older man. His wife, Elena, who appears half mad, pretends to dress elegantly; she often speaks of her success at dances in Rome. Their daughter, Irene, can be heard in the other room. Before they leave Ugo to sleep in an improvised bed, Augusto tells him with a wink to feel as if he were in his own home. If he needs a glass of water, he should go to the end of the hall and get it, not to worry about the person sleeping there.

Alone, Ugo hears Irene coughing to catch his attention. The hall is lit, and she can be seen lying in bed, raised on one elbow, with a fixed smile, the face *"of a doll or of an angel."* Ugo speaks to her, but she only laughs invitingly. Meanwhile a Voice, not heard by Ugo, *"very far away, menacing, and painful"* is heard to say: "The crutches!... Irene hide your crutches,..."[25] and Irene *"maneuvers under the bed to better hide the crutches."* The act ends with Ugo going to Irene's bed.

Ugo is the first "inspector" in Betti's theater who becomes a participant in the action and pathos of the drama. His insertion among the other characters represents another special note in this fable-play. In *Goat Island*, a different kind of fable, Angelo, a foreigner, becomes an integral part of the story. He is an angel of evil, and Agata, the protagonist of that play, ended in despair and Hell; now, Ugo is an angel of mercy, and Irene will die in bliss and go to Paradise.

In Act II, at City Hall, Gregorio, the Mayor, asks Ugo to sign an expulsion order against the city clerk, Augusto; he has been cheating on the accounts. Ugo hesitates, for he has been touched by Irene. He recounts how the night before there was something in her "above all humble, even imploring...that moved and embarrassed.... Then I understood what we call love."[26] The villagers mock him and tell him that Irene is a cripple and that anyone in the village has had or can have her—except Nicola, the narrator. Ugo, horrified, signs the order and runs away.

What has happened to Irene is a story of degradation. When she began to dream of love and nobody wanted her, her father in pity sought anyone who was willing to take her. The first was the mayor, then anyone else, including the mayor's son, Giovanni, who neglects his own wife and family. Augusto's decision, however, may not have resulted from compassion alone, but from greed; perhaps he is not a loving father but, as the villagers believe, a filthy opportunist. Betti wants to leave the point unclear. Elena's attitude toward her daughter also oscillates between cruelty and anguish; it is years since they have spoken, and, when they are in the same room, Elena never looks at Irene. Irene herself appears ambiguous: Is she a morally depraved creature, or a victim of vice and brutality?

However: no matter how ambiguous these protagonists, Betti's interest is not moral or social. Irene is a prostitute *and* a cripple. The author clearly wants the spectator to associate these two circumstances. Each is an unavoidable datum beyond Irene's will. Each represents an existential condition which "finitizes" man and his aspirations for the infinite. When she meets Ugo, Irene's longing to walk without crutches, to be pure, and to be able to marry "in a white dress," as a virgin, are intensified. It must be underlined that it is not a question of repentance; if it were, it would be a pitiful and pathetic case of a wretched person's life. But Irene cannot, and does not have to, repent for her prostitution in the same way she cannot and does not repent for being a cripple. It is interesting and opportune to remember that Betti once observed that if he were to make a play about Don Juan, he would save him without having him repent.[27]

In Act III Ugo is on the mountain road running away from the village. Nicola, the helper of the fable,[28] reaches him to inform him that "strange things" are going on in Irene's house. Ugo goes back. Irene and her parents want to leave, but the villagers are ashamed of their own degrading behavior they cannot do without. A gradual rebellion in feeling is taking place. First Augusto says: "It happens that, at a certain point, one realizes that it is too much. One reaches a point, and one cannot bear it any longer."[29] And Elena with "*an unexpected scream of immense desperation,*" says: "Oh my God. Why do I continue to pretend, while I cannot bear it any longer."[30] Irene crosses the room on her crutches and a few moments later a "*scream and thump*" are heard, as she throws herself out the window. Irene's scream is more "convincingly determined"[31] than Betti's three

other heroines who scream while committing suicide: Adelia in
Night in the Rich Man's House, Laura in *Spiritism in the Ancient
House*, and Elena in *Corruption in the Palace of Justice*. Irene is
the "least schematic"[32] of Betti's "innocent" figures.

The drama has reached its conclusion. Irene's suicide is an
affirmation of freedom. She refuses the indignity of her finitude;
she was not responsible for it, hence innocent. But Betti doesn't
want to end her tragedy with the scream of a cathartic suicide,
and in fact Irene is carried in mortally wounded. The play is a
fable, and in Betti's notes its original title was *Miracle in the
Mountains*.[33] The last two scenes are not a discrepancy, they just
extend the fabulous. Irene deserves to believe the lie—the miracle—that she will be married for the rest of her life to Ugo and
walk like everyone else. There is more than a "shadow" of melo-
drama[34] because the two last scenes are too long. In an opera, the
length of the death scene would be less objectionable.

In spite of the miracle, the end, "apparently happy, actually
is deeply bitter."[35] The finite condition of man cannot be
changed. Irene is able to change it only with her death. Ugo's act
of *caritas* is but the participation in a lie in response to a dying
person's last wish. The villagers are moved by the rite. But their
commotion cannot erase the play's horrific picture of a mean and
stupid society. The fable *is* a fable.

III. Acque turbate

After *Irene innocente*, we would perhaps expect another
effort by Betti to write less pessimistically. One way would have
been to bring "the miracle" within the story of the play instead of
relegating it to the end. This change would have required a less
troubled and more orthodox believer than Betti was, someone
who saw the history of each human being unfolding under the
watchful eye of God. The miracle would have been immanent in
the world in the shape of that Divine Providence which enlivens
Manzoni's *I promessi sposi* (*The Betrothed*). But Betti does not
possess the serene faith of an Alessandro Manzoni; his is the suffering faith of Dante, always aware that sin is not too far away.

In any case, Betti continued to search for the mystery of man's soul, although in his next play, *Acque turbate* (1948; *Troubled Waters*), he seems to be completely overwhelmed by the difficulty of doing good and avoiding evil. As Giovanni Calendoli puts it: "*Troubled Waters* is probably the drama in which Ugo Betti expresses more intensely than in any other his desire to uncover evil and in which he feels more intensely the fatality of a final purification, an extreme elevation beyond earthly life."[36] One can only partially agree with this statement. The drama can easily be viewed outside a theological structure, for it is a tragedy of the impossibility of knowing oneself. This injunction of Greek philosophy is not made easy by Christian faith and is a troubled and troublesome injunction for twentieth century man and artist.

The play also reminds us of ancient Greek theater in its use of a chorus which Betti develops here more than anywhere else, a chorus of two Men [*Tizi*] who, as the author explains, "intervene in various moments of the play. They should have faces as impersonal as possible [maybe this can be emphasized by small identical masks each with an astonished look]."[37] They play two employees, two soldiers, a passerby, a drunkard, a lawyer, a priest, and a sightseer. One critic thinks they "approach in part, the majesty of the chorus of the Greek tragedy."[38] Their entrances are integral parts of the drama, both because they further its action and also because they add to its atmosphere of multilayered reality. The author uses here a device he introduced in *Husband and Wife* — characters speak thoughts aloud which only the audience can hear. In *Troubled Waters* Betti also summons a character onto the stage without realistic preparation, as in *Landslide*, and we also hear voices, as we heard the Voice in *Irene innocente*. The character-narrator Nicola will be represented by the two Men, who are not just narrators but presences; they sketch rather than perform some past action.

In fact, one of the main functions of these Men is to rehearse what happened before the beginning of the play. But their rehearsal is not merely a prologue. The Men come onto the stage and represent visually the memory of the play's coprotagonist, Alda. We could say they choreograph her memory. When we add that the audience is convinced, for a while, that

Alda is trying to free herself of that past, we can perceive how they take an adversary role toward her which transforms the scene into a study in contrast.

Alda is haunted by her past. During the war she was alone in the North, cut off from her family. After the war her brother, Giacomo, found her in a house of prostitution frequented by foreign soldiers. With care and affection he slowly convinced her she wasn't guilty or soiled in any way. Now, at the start of the play, she lives with her brother, his wife and child, in a town where nobody knows about her. She teaches in a little girls' school, and her brother tells her she is as pure as they are. But their peace is interrupted by the arrival of a Commissioner, Gabriele, at the office where Giacomo is director. It is a purge: Giacomo has compromised himself during the previous regime, and Gabriele wants to transfer him to the North. Giacomo tells him of Alda and that for her sake he cannot go. The Commissioner is not moved. Unbeknownst to her husband, Edvige, Giacomo's wife, convinces the attractive Alda to intercede for her brother. Alda becomes the commissioner's mistress.

In the scene in which Alda goes to Gabriele's house, Betti uses one of the Men to reveal her situation to us. As she walks along, this Man comments on her sexual attractiveness as if she were a prostitute, though only the audience sees and hears him. He represents what Alda feels — not only that she is forced to go to Gabriele but also that she really prefers to be a prostitute. When she becomes aware of the Man and speaks to him, he doesn't mock her; in fact, he seems to represent part of herself, almost her conscience. He asks her why she is going to Gabriele, and when she denies she is going, he calls her a liar. When she admits it, she excuses herself by saying: "I must go to save Giacomo! (*Vaguely*) My dear Giacomo, my adored brother...Oh, I must never forget what Giacomo tells me: that I am a little girl, I am like one of my pupils...."[39] The Man laughs at these words, and again he starts commenting on her beauty. This scene implies that there is some kind of ambivalence within Alda and within her relation to her brother, all of which will become clearer in Act II.

From the looks and hints of his colleagues, Giacomo suspects the reason why Gabriele has changed his mind about transferring him. So he invites Gabriele to dinner at his home with the hope and intention of having him reveal himself as the brutal and cynical man he really is in front of Alda. After that (he imagines) sweet and pure Alda will certainly leave him. At dinner, as Giacomo starts speaking of Alda's experience in the North, the two Men, as two colored soldiers, appear and sit at the table; they will stay on stage during the scenes in Giacomo's house. They speak only to each other, and (we perceive) they speak adversely and mockingly of Alda. Giacomo recounts how she was forced by the brutality of her circumstances to do what she did and how afterwards with his help and love she became modest and pure again. We can believe that Alda tried to redeem herself, but the presence of the two Men is too close and prevents us from believing that she has really changed. It seems as if her own presence, wherever she may be, attracts their presence; they are part of what she was and is. We could say they represent her destiny — if we accept Hegel's definition of it as one's own self in an adversary role. In fact, when Gabriele challenges Giacomo's words and hints that Alda was not "forced" to go into "that house," Signora Ines, the madame, appears out of nowhere (like Madama Pace in *Six Characters in Search of an Author* some twenty-seven years before) and says: "By herself, [she came] willingly. Happy."[40] And as long as she remains on stage, she will interpolate, "*whispering, as a refrain*," into the lines of the other characters, "By herself"[41] — though only the audience will see and hear her.

Gabriele leaves the house, and Alda cannot help running after him. She meets him in front of a bar and humbly begs him to take her back; he insults her and hits her. Alda just laughs. Giacomo arrives and Gabriele leaves. Her brother tries to speak to her, but she answers the horrified Giacomo with the expressions of vice and vulgarity; she will go back to her lover tomorrow. After Alda is gone, a far-away voice asks Giacomo three times: "What will you do."[42]

Up to now Alda has never changed into what her brother, and maybe she herself, thought she was. But now, inexorably, she is drawn back into what she always really wanted to be. Her conscious desires don't count. While she has not been sure of herself — her subconscious truth, represented by the Men, was always on the verge of overpowering her — Giacomo is quite self-assured of himself and his ideals. His only worry is about his sister, although he doesn't know what to think or do.

The last scene of Act II begins with him "*stammering*: Help. Help. Help. Help."[43] His plea is answered by human and divine agents. The Men appear, one as a lawyer, the other as a priest. The former tells him that in regard to the law "as a brother he doesn't have any right."[44] When Giacomo turns to the other Man and asks about the intervention of God, if He has "any suggestion," the priest answers: "But it is our duty...to decide, to choose."[45] Then he adds in a strangely unchristian tone: "Doesn't it imply a certain abuse to involve oneself in other people's affairs, even of a sister?... What is it, this doing all one can for others?... There is always something irregular in this.... We are only responsible for our own soul."[46] At the end of the scene, after Edvige and Aglae, Gabriele's wife, have also appeared without bringing any help, the lawyer, more strangely than the priest, says: "At times the best thing for a loved one is for her to die."[47]

Giacomo doesn't take either the priest's or the lawyer's advice. He wants to avenge himself and to free Alda by killing Gabriele. He plans an excursion to a point in the mountains with a very high overhang, called The Balcony, and he takes the two lovers there. Climbing ahead of them, he meets one of the Men in the role of a sightseer coming down who tells him mysteriously: "This evening we'll meet again and you'll tell me everything."[48]

On The Balcony he tells Gabriele that the guilty must be punished, but Gabriele retorts that "Everyone is what he is."[49] Giacomo wants to save Alda and recounts a recurring dream which shows how she is in danger: a hand is playing with her; it outlines "caresses in the air, signs...grabbing...vague...vulgar... obscene."[50] In the dream Alda laughs and tries to run away, then turns, smiles, and winks. She cannot run because, breathless, she is hampered by "her knees,...hair, skirts, chest, hips...thick hips, heavy breasts, heavy thighs..."[51] In his self-assurance, Giacomo interprets the dream as if the hand were Gabriele's. He means to free his sister of him, and afterwards help her again to chastity and virtue. Alda rebels, telling him she doesn't want to be helped by him. She feels "sincere and true" with Gabriele even if he insults her. Giacomo has tormented her enough. Her brother doesn't believe her. Gabriele laughs and tells him he is a liar just as one of the Men had called Alda a liar when she was "pretending" to be a teacher in Act I. Finally Gabriele explains: "There is also a big worm in you. The biggest. You are the only one keeping your eyes closed...that hand...of your dream...that was going near your sister...it wasn't mine. Giacomo, your affection for your sister is too much."[52] Giacomo shocked, besides himself, enraged, slips and falls from The Balcony.

At this point Betti introduces the most original and daring device in his *oeuvre*. Theatrically, it is a stroke of genius. The last scenes of the play take place while Giacomo is falling down the side of the mountain, trying to stop his fall by grabbing "*tufts of grass and chips of rock.*" During these last seconds of life, Giacomo screams, "No," and a Man appears, the same one he spoke to on climbing the mountain, who told him they would meet again. The Man asks him why he doesn't consent to die. Giacomo answers: "Because everything has been misunderstood, distorted...I myself, right then and there, was confused. That's why I fell."[53] Gabriele, Edvige, and Aglae appear, though not Alda since, as the Man says, those "words were enough to change her, to burn her...she will always run."[54] Giacomo confesses that he feels "all muddied...ashamed of *his* eyes, of *his* thoughts, of *his* sighs...."[55] When Gabriele says he uttered those words to defend himself, Giacomo is no longer interested in Gabriele's denial. To have believed them for a moment made them true. He is ready to die.

The last scene is between Giacomo and the Man. Giacomo realizes that he hadn't known himself: he *was* a liar. He asks himself: "Was I the worst?... How could such an unwanted evil be born and grow in me, without my knowing it? And how is it possible that I, without wanting it, must be responsible?"[56] His conclusion is what must have been for Betti a very disturbing line to write: "Perhaps it is the fact itself, existence itself, which has been dirty since the beginning."[57] The Man exhorts him to be trusting—the "troubled waters" will quiet down. Giacomo takes his hand off the grass and lets himself fall. Now Alda appears and asks the Man to tell her brother that everything will be explained and that they will go to Paradise holding hands, as they wanted to do when they were children. The Man replies in the play's last line: "He knows."[58]

There lurks a dark irony in this line. For Giacomo is the man who lived a lie all his life—who didn't know himself and his incestuous desire, who didn't really know his wife, and who didn't know his sister who enjoyed being a prostitute. In this drama the real protagonist is Giacomo's subconscious in its demonic force. There is no God, not even at the end. The Man comforts dying Giacomo with a lyrical description of a soothing evening: "The freshness of evening already comes to the leaves.... The crescent moon has just begun to shine.... The world is peaceful."[59] Again Betti's characters are in the dark wood. We don't see in this play the "purification" of which Calendoli[60] speaks. Perhaps there is a desire for one, but also the sad conviction that it is impossible to achieve it.

Several critics, among them Cologni,[61] Calendoli,[62] and Apollonio,[63] are of the opinion that *Troubled Waters* is Betti's "masterpiece." The play is certainly one of his best for the theatrical inventiveness which successfully brings into focus the protagonists's agon, an agon which is tragic in the precariousness and vulnerability of Giacomo's unstoppable fall (*descensus*).

IV. The Queen and the Rebels

The self-sacrifice and redemption of the prostitute after Dumas, Dostoyevsky, and Tolstoy, is a common literary metaphor for representing the power of goodness inherent in human beings. Love and religion are usually the catalysts of this reversal. In one of his myth-plays, *The New Colony*, Pirandello makes a symbol of a redeemed prostitute, La Spera, who remains alone with her baby while the world around her sinks into the sea. But La Spera regains her purity not through love or religion but motherhood and the desire for the respectability society has denied her. Betti's prostitute-character also rebels against those social humiliations which have rendered her a means to other people's pleasure, and in the name of human dignity she transforms herself into a queen. But unlike Pirandello's La Spera, Betti's Argia is not presented as merely symbolic but as a realistic figure who is transformed from a shameless and abject nonentity into a desperately self-aware and proud human being.

In fact, Argia, the protagonist of *La Regina e gli Insorti* (1949; *The Queen and the Rebels*, 1956), seems psychologically more believable than all the other characters in the drama. This difference is the more striking if one considers the fact that this is a political play, one of the two in which Betti deals with the politics and the historical experiences of postwar Italy. Indeed, the "committed" rebels are so stylized that they may at times appear ridiculous caricatures of revolutionaries. The reason is that Betti is not finally interested in social questions: his ultimate artistic concern is man facing the ultimate questions.

The view of the new social order or of the dynamics of revolution expressed by the rebels is too simplistic even for demagogy. The Communist revolutionaries display such a ferocious, hence comical, attitude towards their adversaries and their fellow men that the spectator is compelled to explain, not accept, them. One critic, Ruggero Jacobbi, believes that Betti "attributes to Marxism arguments and psychological tones typically Nazist,"[64] and he adds that "one doesn't know how much of it is done in good faith."[65] This seems a gratuitous imputation of political chicanery. Betti's lack of direct political commitment is reflected in all his artistic output: whenever there is a reference to an historical situation in his theater, it is sublimated.

The Queen and the Rebels must also not be ideologically interpreted as a mirror of the author's thought. Its atrocities and cynicism represent that "natural course of events" of which Sartre writes and which "sometimes throws us into [inescapable] deadlocks."[66] What matters in this play is the birth of self-consciousness in an individual and how he will face those deadlocks his condition suggests. Again the only realistic character in the play projects a certain ambivalence or rather a bivalence towards realism and metaphor, and one can see a precedent for her in Maria, the protagonist of one of Betti's first plays, *An Inn on the*

Harbor, who also suffers humiliation in quest of a more dignified existence. In 1930 Betti needed to convert Maria through the power of motherhood; now Argia faces herself in her existential "nakedness."[67] No vision of the ideal helps her toward self-realization as a free and responsible agent. Argia represents what many other protagonists of Betti's theater in part represented before her, an attempt to answer the question: What is a man? Apropos of this play John Gatt-Rutter writes: "So closed was Betti's mind to concrete social analysis that he could present a person's real identity only in the extraordinary situation of *La Regina e gli Insorti,* and then only by having everybody mistake that person for someone at the opposite end of the social scale."[68]

The events of the play take place during a revolution in an unidentified country, in a hillside village near the border.[69] People are fleeing the country, and some travellers are stopped by the rebels for interrogation. They are looking for the wife of the ex-dictator, known as The Queen, who escaped their killing five years ago. She has become a legend among a large part of the population, and she knows the names of the rebels' most important enemies. She is a great threat to the new order because a counterrevolution could be mounted around her. In this group of travellers are Argia, who is looking for her lover Raim, and The Queen, disguised as a peasant woman.

Raim, in fact, is one of the rebels they meet, but when he is alone with Argia, he rejects her entreaties. She is, he says, a slut who would be a hindrance to his plans: "I want to come through all the mess alive. And rich."[79] Raim's idea is that "one side's going to come out on top after all this; and if you've been robbing and betraying and murdering on that side you'll be a hero; if you've done the same for the other you'll be ruined."[71] Argia begs him to keep her with him, since in the city in which she was living she felt like "a rat, a drowned rat."[72] She was afraid, alone, and lonely — that's why she came looking for him. Raim is not moved; she would be "only a dead weight," and, besides, she has "too many wrinkles for *his* liking." Argia, "*trying to turn the whole thing into a jest*," says: "A few minutes ago, when they were all talking about the Queen...they all looked at me. They half thought I was the Queen."[73] Raim answers: "The Queen! There isn't a square inch about you that's decent." Near the end of the first act, alone with The Queen in disguise, she comments: "I find it rather humiliating being a woman. Even rather humiliating being alive."[74] As the act ends, she recognizes The Queen in disguise, and with this piece of news intends to tie Raim to her again.

In Act II, while robbing The Queen and eliciting from her the names of her important friends for purposes of blackmail, Argia also comes to know who The Queen really is. Previously she had heard people speak of her as a superior being respected even by some of her enemies. Amos himself, for example, the Commissary who wants to capture her, had said: "The only human needs she [The Queen] ever seems to have acknowledged were the ones that can be reconciled with a dignified and honorable idea of the world."[75] A few minutes after hearing these words, Raim tells Argia: "If ever there was a filthy creature in the world, you're it."[76] There couldn't be a greater contrast. But now Argia discovers that The Queen actually has been living for the past five years as a "terrified animal running this way and that."[77] She has given herself to any man who looked at her suspiciously, for she cares only to go on living, she is frightened of torture.

In the first act, The Queen heard the guard Maupa say: "We want to see the color of the Queen's entrails.... If she falls into my hands, I'll keep her dying slowly for three whole days."[78] When Argia sees The Queen kneeling in front of her, she feels a kind of betrayal because she too would like to believe in a noble queen. Argia *"with gloomy hostility,"* tells her: "It's dishonorable, it's unfair, to lose your dignity like this.... [It] embarrasses people. A chambermaid would behave better. I would myself, my dear."[79] This is the first sign of change in Argia; she is surprised, outraged at The Queen's baseness and fear, and we are surprised at her surprise. Later she feels pity and helps The Queen run away.

Argia has confronted herself, for The Queen's behavior before her in the second act is the same shameless, frightened, and humiliating behavior she displayed before Raim in the first. Argia's behavior, in fact, seems worse because The Queen's abjectness was caused by the circumstance of pursuit.

In Act III, when Argia is accused of being The Queen, she takes it in jest. Notwithstanding the fact that she knows The Queen is not at all a noble figure, she is amused by the mix-up because she is convinced that surely no one could mistake her, a prostitute, for the noble person The Queen is or is expected to be. Nevertheless, in this act, we witness Argia's metamorphosis from prostitute to Queen: she becomes what she wanted all her life to be by assuming the role she is playing. It is a Pirandellian feat. (In the same manner Baldovino is transformed in *The Pleasure of Honesty*.) Amos tells her: "If you're not the Queen...you give a very good imitation of the haughty way in which she'd behave on an occasion like this."[80] Argia, who still thinks she can prove who she is by calling Raim as a witness, answers: "The reason is that I've been rehearsing this role for a very long time." At the end of the act both the real queen and Raim are dead, and Argia finds herself trapped forever in her role, just as another Pirandellian character, "Henry IV," is.

Betti could have concluded the drama at the end of the third act with Amos' pronouncement: "The revolution has decided that the Queen must die. The sentence will be carried out during the course of the night."[81] It would have been a fitting end, but Betti preferred to add a fourth act, the only fourth act in his *oeuvre*. The reason for the extra act is not to show the rebels' intention of keeping The Queen "alive and in disgrace," after she supposedly reveals her high-placed friends. Nor is it to present the melodramatic scene with the child of the real queen who, they tell Argia, is going to be killed if she doesn't tell those names. Nor is it to present the "miracle" of a mental block which prohibits her from remembering those names. Neither is it to reveal Argia's achieved self-awareness, her dignity and freedom: "I am not afraid any longer. My face expresses dignity. I am as I would always have wished to be.... It would have been enough to want to be.... It was my own fault."[82] After all, she could have made this speech just before exiting at the end of Act III. These additions don't further Argia's *askesis* and therefore seem supernumerary.

What makes this act valid and coherent, both within this drama and within all of Betti's theatrical production, is the revelation of Amos' world-vision and the final contrast between Argia and Amos. "The revolution turns out in the end to spring from a hitherto unconscious rage for destruction, for total negation of an intolerable world."[83] Amos' revolutionary zeal, as he proclaims it, is the "distillation of a very different grief...[one which] says 'no' to everything there is.... It says the world is wrong, it's all absurdity; an immense, unchangeable quarry of despair, a grotesque...labyrinth of injustice, an insensate clockwork...total sterilization."[84] Amos' speech should put to rest any discussion of Betti's interest — as an artist — in depicting Communists or revolutionaries in general,[85] and it is not just a refusal of commitment but "it is, on the contrary," in the words of Lucienne Portier, "a matter of a much deeper and total commitment, not limited to a particular and passing event."[86] Betti's is the revolution of the underground man.

But more important, Amos' speech brings the drama to a higher climax. The contrast now is between chaos and annihilation on the one hand, freedom and affirmation on the other. His speech is an apotheosis of death, while Argia's acceptance of cathartic death is an apotheosis of life and "an invitation to redemption."[87] It is this contrast which, in the words of Brooks Atkinson, gives "Betti's dark drama a sublime conclusion."[88]

V. The Gambler

Il giocatore (1950; *The Gambler*, 1966) is a complex play, the main focus of which is the familiar Bettian obsession with responsibility for one's actions and intentions. Betti stresses it now in developing the struggle of the play's protagonist: in fact, it claims too much of our attention, and overshadows the drama's main concern. In other pieces we have seen secondary characters exist as functions of the protagonist: their pretenses helped throw light on deeper layers of the protagonist's self. For example, in *Husband and Wife*, (another play, like *The Gambler*, about a married couple), Signora Erminia, Olga's sister, and even the young Filippo, who causes the breakup of the marriage, are important only insofar as they build out the space in which Luigi and Olga live their experience. The same differentiation between protagonist and the other characters is also true of *Struggle Till Dawn*: Giorgio always remains in the foreground of our attention; his wife Elsa and the other couple, Tullio and Delia, no matter how much involved they are in the plot — physically and emotionally — remain in the background of Giorgio's struggle.

In *The Gambler* two of the minor characters — instead of just playing accessory parts in relation to the protagonist, Ennio — become protagonists themselves in their relationship to Ennio's dead wife Iva. Ermete, Ennio's lawyer, becomes so involved in the drama that at a certain point he becomes the "plaintiff" himself. What he reveals about Iva, her lovable side, is important, since it shows how Ennio was blind to her, and it also points to the problem of identity in regard to Iva. In the scene when he prepares the flower-bed of Iva's tomb, he becomes the protagonist. Alma's intervention has a collateral dramatic interest, for she too has a private life worth exploring in relation to her sister Iva and to Ennio; we learn that her denunciation of Ennio is caused not by affection for her sister and love of justice but mainly by envy for her. Her envy is not subordinate to the development of Ennio's story.

Iva is not a minor character as Elsa is in *Struggle Till Dawn*; at the least, she has the same stature as Olga in *Husband and Wife*. But in this latter drama Betti's intention is to explore the relationship of a couple as the play's title clearly implies; in *The Gambler* the playwright's main concern is to explore Ennio's "bets" with destiny, his taking "risks," his success in avoiding responsibility. However, his dead wife's presence and complex personality (as revealed to us in her letters to her sister), the love she arouses in Ermete, and her appearance as a character on stage — an appearance which is not limited to the audience's eyes as dead Olga's is, for Iva enters in conversation with Ennio — give the play a second focus of interest, a husband-wife tension. This collateral interest is relevant in that it expands the play: *The Gambler* is more than just another "struggle" towards salvation. Jean Anouilh was attracted mainly by this aspect of the drama and wrote that it is "one of the subtler, stronger, and more disquieting variations on the theme of that encounter between two solitudes that is called a couple. Who is that man who can be sure of having known his own wife? Who is that man who can be sure of not having killed her a little, by killing her last possibility of issuing from her sack of skin? *The Gambler* answers this question."[89] If we also add the question, Who is that wife who can be certain of having known her husband? we can perceive how forceful and relevant this aspect of the play is.

There are, however, the play's other sides which also claim our attention. If Anouilh sensed one main theme and succeeded in abstracting it, professional theater critics in the United States were not as able to penetrate the complexity of the drama. Nevertheless, Brooks Atkinson in *The New York Times* considered it a "puzzle,"[90] and Walcott Gibbs, critic of *The New Yorker*, judged it an "Italian cryptogram," an example of a "vacant and pretentious art work."[91] Seven years later Atkinson would write in *The New York Times* that *The Gambler* "conveyed a sense of spiritual responsibility that had to be respected."[92] We don't know to what extent Betti's play — his first to be done professionally in New York — was "adapted" for American audiences, but it is one of his most difficult.

The reason is that the author was largely interested in form for its own sake. As Di Pietro observes, after reading the unpublished notes for *The Gambler*, "it is more an attempt to find new ways of expression for his theater than to express something."[93] In the notes Betti writes of his desire to create a "free scheme."[94] Already in *Troubled Waters*, he had used a staging technique in which the props necessary for a scene or part of a scene would be illuminated while unnecessary props would be left in darkness. In *The Gambler* Betti also introduces "meaningful objects"[95] which become integral and suggestive parts of the drama's direction. A yellow satin bedspread comes to represent Iva's willing submission and her sexual advances to Ennio; Iva's ghost emerges from a mahogany-colored closet; a scarlet-colored armchair represents divine judgment. Iva wears a wedding gown every time she appears in spite of the fact that she never wore it in her life, not even on her wedding day; a torn and hanging piece of the skirt symbolizes Iva's fatal destiny in marriage.

Betti also makes use of this theatrical element in the figure of the Railroad Official in his *"black cap heavily fringed in gold"* who appears seated on a scarlet-colored armchair as a personage of divine justice. Furthermore, as he had done twenty years before in *Landslide*, Betti introduces dead persons on stage. Finally, critics[96] also note a filmic technique in the changing of scenes, one fading while a new one comes to view.

At the beginning of the play Betti conjures up a befogged railroad station through *"signal lights and an illuminated clock,"* whistles, and the sounds of trains. Ennio has just arrived and is met by a Railroad Official, an important figure in the play, who will later be transformed into the divine representative. Ennio has come because a semiofficial investigation is being conducted. His sister-in-law, Alma, has accused him of having caused the death of his wife—at the hands of "irregular" troops—during the late war. Ermete has taken his case, one of those "confusing accidents...[the] authorities would prefer to let the distant and sensitive scales of [the] Supreme Being weigh...and in the meantime settle [them] in a discreet manner."[97] Ennio didn't do anything directly to cause Iva's death, even if he felt (he tells Ermete) "awfully glad when it happened,"[98] for he was tired of her, her love, her submission; in fact he had wished to get rid of her. Ermete interrupts him to state that he, Ennio, is a "gambler and [he is] overstaking the throw."[99] He shouldn't express certain things, and he should even try to slander Iva. Ennio refuses. He tried his luck by sowing "the ground, with the most innocent of seeds.... But it happened. Because the flaw was not in the seeds but in the soil: in the soul."[100] He communicated his desires to his mistress Piera, but how could he have imagined her "capable of distilling the iciest of poison from the most innocuous words"?[101] Piera informed against him; failing to capture him, the troops took Iva and killed her.

In the second act Ennio convinces Alma to withdraw her accusations. She does—she was acting out of envy for her sister who always had more attention since they were children. Besides, when they first met, Ennio looked at her, not Iva. Alma and Ennio make love.

Ermete reveals while he is fixing the flower-bed on Iva's grave that he loved her and that they would have been married if Ennio had not come along. Beautiful Iva's ghost is sitting in front of the grave. Ermete knows everything about Ennio and he adds as a conclusion: "You have confessed everything. And to top it off, we've let you go unpunished. My job was precisely this: to reveal you down to the last dregs and then see you leave unpunished."[102] Ennio is defiant, and when he starts to leave, Ermete tells him that Iva preferred to die rather than inform the "irregulars" where her husband was. Ennio is overcome, Iva's ghost picks up a flower from her grave and offers it to him. As the act ends, Dr. Pinci, the Commissioner, Alma and Piera, arrive and Ennio—as the scene fades out and the scarlet-armchair appears—tells him: "Wait, Commissioner. Before you decide...I still have one more thing to tell you."[103]

The scenes between Ennio and Alma, and Ennio and Ermete in the second act are too long, and introduce into the play what we may call dispersive elements. Yet Betti presents us with particular inquiries into two human beings.

In Act III Dr. Pinci is ready to close the case, but Ennio, shocked by Ermete's revelation, doesn't want to be acquitted "on the basis of truth." As a gambler, he wants to take another chance. Alma and Piera don't complain, but Iva does. Dr. Pinci, however, is not ready to punish: "You think you killed her only because you wanted to kill her. It's just your conscience. I thought so. It's not a crime.... Acquitted!"[104] But, immediately after, the Railroad Official who is present only to the audience adds: "Condemned." Iva appears and Ennio, in a symbolic gesture, kills her again. The play ends at the station. Ennio is free to go in accord with human justice. Piera, Ermete, Dr. Pinci, and Alma call him "murderer." The Official tells him: "The game's over. There's no trick that will help you now.... Tremble at last."[105] But Ennio has a last card to play. His faith in a loving God is so sure that he can gamble on the certainty that He cannot be less loving and forgiving than one of his creatures; if Iva forgives him, God will too for all eternity. He explains: "I knew I would be able to cheat my way out of it!"[106] He calls Iva and she answers. He is saved. The Official addresses God in rather heterodox fashion: "You untiring and loving Judge. You, regal injustice, sublime condescension.... You...make human creatures and allow them to face up to You and for this You love them."[107]

A friend of Betti, the critic Giovanni Calendoli, recounts that the last lines of the Official "cost Betti much painful work: days and days of rethinking, of correction, of multiple versions, of words and adjectives now added, now erased."[108] While other plays which deal with salvation, like *Corruption in the Palace of Justice* and *Troubled Waters*, end on a note of hope, *The Gambler* ends with absolute certainty of faith in God and salvation. In the words of the critic Gildo Moro, "Betti in [this] drama arrives at a moment where guilt, forgiveness and justice, good and evil are overcome, burned in one immense pyre which is God's love."[109]

As we observed earlier the play lacks a central focus toward which the other elements converge; Betti's hand was taken over by his desire to experiment with stage techniques, which are striking but do not coalesce with the concerns of the play. Perhaps the best comment on it is the one made by Brooks Atkinson, who didn't much like the play, yet felt compelled to admire its fresh stagecraft.[110]

VI. The Burnt Flower-Bed

The Queen and the Rebels was Betti's first political play; *L'aiuola bruciata* (1951-52; *The Burnt Flower-Bed*, 1958) is his other.[111] This play also brings two worlds together, for it too is constructed of two vectors inextricably influencing each other: politics and the person, society and the individual, history and man. Again Betti is not interested in merely presenting a political situation or political ideas; in fact, the plot develops mainly through the intimate experiences of some of the characters, not through political involvement. However, the two vectors seem not to have a point of convergence; throughout the play—until the very surprising end—they go into opposite directions. One tendency representing politics, society, and history pushes forward toward the future; the other, involving man in his individuality, goes backward toward the past and the psychic reality of man. The first is based on outward action, the forging of a new and better order of things; the second on inward action, on an obsessive

Bettian digging into the past, into something that happened five years before — the same time lapse of *Struggle Till Dawn* — in an effort to explain it and assign responsibility.

This tension, which constantly vibrates throughout the drama, lends it its dynamic structure. If this central dynamism is misunderstood, the play will be distorted and will not be able to convey its meaning — meaning which is not political in spite of the long dialogues and confrontation about history and revolution. History and revolution, in other words, must be taken not (or not only) for the meanings they obviously declare but for what they symbolize in the structural economy of the drama, the faceless statistical group which has the power to overwhelm and even annihilate its single member with his singular beauty — the flower-bed.

Owing to his gift for oratory Giovanni, the protagonist, had become one of the leaders of the revolution; but intraparty squabbles forced him to abandon politics. He exiled himself and his wife to a house in the mountains near the frontier. The living room of this house is the setting for the whole play, but it is enlarged by the distant view of "*high peaks of snow-covered mountains,*" seen through some arched doors. It reminds us of the setting of *The Queen and the Rebels*, which also takes place near the border. Both plays last from sunset to dawn.

The border divides two political regimes with entirely opposite ideologies. Giovanni's ex-comrades (Tomaso and Nicola) fear the influence of the other side. Something must be done. Tomaso, one of the current leaders, has come to visit Giovanni who is now a legend among the people, more popular than any of the current leaders because of his self-imposed exile. Luisa, Giovanni's wife, who behaves very strangely, informs Tomaso that the reason for their exile was not politics but the death of their fifteen year old son Guido and that in the last five years Giovanni has not been the same because both she and her husband cannot accept the casualness of such a cruelly fatal accident: Guido falling out of a window.

Tomaso's plan is to send a delegation to the border to sue for reconciliation: it will be an act of good will noticed by the newspapers in both countries. War can be avoided. Giovanni should lead the delegation—since he is so admired his presence would lend more dignity to the enterprise. But Giovanni refuses: he is no longer interested in politics. In order to convince him Tomaso introduces Rosa, the daughter of Andrea the Baker whom the rebels long ago shot on Giovanni's order during one of their first demonstrations against the old regime. This staged "incident" provided the necessary spark that set the revolution on its course to victory. Since Giovanni gave the command then, he has now an obligation to himself and the revolution. He cannot betray that dead man and his daughter who is dedicating herself to nursing the very sick Nicola, the most important leader of the revolutionary party, the one who took Giovanni's place.

The mixture of public and private interests continues in Act II, which is largely divided into two confrontations: one, between Giovanni on one side, Tomaso and Raniero on the other; the other, between Giovanni and Nicola. The first deals with Giovanni's relation to the revolution, the second with his obsessive concern for his son's death. To Tomaso he explains he is not willing to participate in the peace mission because he doesn't believe any longer in his oratory. He went into isolation, he says, because "speeches were making *him* ill."[112] He wonders what the teenage Guido who was always present at his speeches thought of them. Is there a link between his oratory and the death of his son?

Anyhow, "the reason a political leader wants to change the people is that the people as they are disgust him."[113] Giovanni adds that "'us and them' are really one and the same thing."[114] Each leader "should apologize...to everyone. The people."[115] In conclusion Giovanni's vision of man is bitter: "The distinctive human product is folly, and man is only a garden for its cultivation. Sheep can have offspring, as we can; horses can draw carts, as we can; but *folly*—only man is capable of that."[116] But his view lifts man out of the faceless and statistical, a view of man that a revolutionary of the kind his collegues suppose he is cannot hold. Giovanni states: "There's a kind of epidemic in the world. When people are all together, they don't notice it.... Everyone [is] happy. Then they go back home.... Sad. *Bos. Pecus*.... They feel...stupefied.... They go and look at themselves in the mirror....

They don't believe they're real."[117] The reason for this is that men are not "wholly satisfied...all that progress merely means [that men are] dying fatter, cleaner, better dressed."[118]

Betti's revolutionaries are always of a special kind.[119] When Giovanni sees himself acting, when he imagines how he is perceived by Guido, or when he sees himself in the mirror of his own self-awareness, he cannot continue to act spontaneously and to believe in his action. Like Pirandello's Viteangelo Moscarda in *One, None and a Hundred Thousand*, he can either live or see himself living. When Giovanni starts reflecting, he takes man out of "crowded squares, [and] crowded stadiums," and considers him in his existential anguish. We must hasten to add that we don't believe Giovanni's reasoning makes the play "too dense in concepts and in theses to be demonstrated which dilute the poetic tone and burden the action."[120] In fact, Giovanni's vision of man outside time and space is presented in vivid contrast to a vision of a progressive path in human history. This is a scene from the theater of ideas. But what raises Giovanni's words out of the merely conceptual and renders them instead rather poignant is the fact that his change of heart and of belief are prompted by his son's tragic accident.

In his confrontation with Nicola, Giovanni feels free to speak to the dying man of his dead son. He confesses his lack of communication with Guido. His oratory, so forceful and communicative with the crowd, was not useful in reaching his son who was "asking...for an explanation.... He wanted to tell him... who he was, what he wanted. But *he* [Giovanni] hadn't the patience, *he* didn't pay attention...[although] he [Guido] is the only person *he has* ever loved."[121] The father couldn't prevent Guido's death. Nor was he able to explain to him what should be explained to all, that "everyone is...very great, very important.... Every man must be persuaded—even if he is in rags—that he is immensely, immensely important!"[122] With these anti-revolutionary revolutionary beliefs Giovanni decides to lead the delegation for peace.

Before the act ends, Rosa tells him that the meeting is only a trick; Tomaso is planning another "incident," like the one of Andrea the Baker. They plan to kill Giovanni as he steps out of the house and blame "the others" across the border; then they will be justified in declaring war. Giovanni is tempted to run, but his wife Luisa, in her madness, feels she cannot bear alone the burden of Guido's accident. She still wants "just to understand one particular thing. Nothing happens without a reason for it"[123]; she believes "that someone must have been responsible, there couldn't not have been someone. It would have been absurd."[124] She doesn't want to let Giovanni escape and she calls Tomaso, but Giovanni comes back by himself. We don't know why. Act I ended with Giovanni's refusal to participate in a mission of peace; Act II with his acceptance of death in a staged "incident." To this one must add that Guido's death is also unresolved. One has the feeling that not all has been made clear yet. Is there a connection between Guido's accident and this "accident" in which his father will be the victim? And what about Andrea the Baker's "accident"?

The last act will bring these three accidents together. In the first part of Act III Betti strips Tomaso of his exterior as a dutiful son of the revolution. As at the end of *The Queen and the Rebels*, in which Amos is revealed as an anguished man fighting in vain, here too Betti presents us with a revolutionary — a Communist, some critics believe — whose ideas and deeds are not dictated by the tenets of ideology but by a soul-felt vision of himself as a puny entity in the midst of others. When Giovanni asks him if he believes, Tomaso, who now feels he can be "sincere" and "free" since dawn is approaching and perhaps he too will be killed, is ready "to reveal a secret" and confesses that although he has spent a whole lifetime in the revolution, he admits that "I've never done anything!... Action is a dream! We see hands move: and they're not ours. The gestures of a dream."[125] Amos spent his life expressing his rage, Tomaso accepts the universe convinced that man can add "nothing" to it. Whatever happens doesn't depend "on us. Only on itself."[126] Nothing can be wrong, if "grass, grubs in the earth...know nothing of right and wrong.... [In] what way do [men] differ from them? Life...everything obeys it. And children fall and die.... That is the fate of everything.... [Why] should man be the only exception?"[127]

In this "political" play the contrast at the end is also lifted beyond any social question. Giovanni will object that all other things in the universe "are not aware of the fact [that they are wearing away while] there is one tiny character that knows that... That's where the great torment stings; and it squeezes...the drop of acid."[128] This is the reason, we are finally told, Guido died. He didn't just "obey" life by falling out of the window. Giovanni reveals that he jumped from it. He must have felt that "the world is diseased...a vast, blighted flower-bed,"[129] and he couldn't and didn't accept it. At dawn Giovanni will reenact Guido's suicide. He projects upon his son his own terror of life—of which he spoke in Act II—and imagines Guido with an "empty look...of one whose only fate is to die. Purposeless: unenduring, unredeemable: an error."[130] Guido's death was not an accident and neither will Giovanni's be. He says: "It's I who want it. This error has to be punished."[131]

To Tomaso's naturalistic conception of man, Giovanni contraposes man as an unhappy thinking reed aware of being a reed, "destitute," in his words, "of title to any kind of pride and hope."[132] However, at the conclusion of this last long scene young Rosa emerges as an important part of the drama's conclusion. She will redeem her father's brutish death by running out of the door first because, as she says: "I do not believe that they will really shoot... that people want to kill."[133] She does it also as an answer to Guido's despair. Like Argia she wants to affirm hope and life messianically: "Oh, what grace was given us when we were called on to exist and to see."[134] On the threshold she is shot, and with her body in his arms Giovanni starts walking towards the border trusting, like Rosa, that "they will not shoot.... [Now] they will respect us."[135] Tomaso and Raniero assent and follow him. No shots are heard, and, in fact, the signal of musical bugle-calls now has "*a festive sound*."[136]

The play ends in hope and dignity like *The Queen and the Rebels*; in both there is a cathartic sacrifice. However, there is a substantial difference between Argia and Rosa as theatrical figures. The former is a well-developed character; her collusion with Amos' dark view of the universe, and her conclusive acceptance of death, though pregnant with symbolic meaning, coalesces well with the past development of the play. There couldn't be a play, let alone an ending, without Argia. Rosa, on the other hand, seems to be a willed addition, something of a *deus ex machina*. As if her presence were more necessary to Betti than to the play. Perhaps it is so. Her strength of character and of spiritual involvement at the end are surprising. But for her to convey her meaning, we must see her within a different frame than we see Argia. Rosa's presence is constructive rather than representational; she doesn't develop a real personal relationship with the other characters and she rarely speaks until just before the end because Betti is not interested in delineating character. Her only distinguishing feature is the innocence of her youth, and as innocence she is Betti's reaction to both Tomaso's and Giovanni's circles of Hell. Rosa is a stage projection of the author's unconscious: a conceptualized possibility, a longed-for need, of an existence in a non-hell.

VII. The Fugitive

Betti completed *La fuggitiva* (1952–53; *The Fugitive*, 1964) a few months before his death. It is imprudent and risky to speculate on what would have happened if his end had been less untimely, but we tend to believe that with *The Fugitive* he had reached a turning point in his career. This last play introduces a new and different intellectual attitude, and it shows us a greater ease in handling some theatrical devices Betti had been experimenting with all along.

The constant feature of Betti's serious theater, as we have seen, takes the form of an inquisitive probing, official or unofficial, into a character, relationship, or situation; at its resolution we participate in a discovery or self-discovery which at times brings salvation, at times a desire for redemption, at other times damnation. In any case, we are always nearing a gaping abyss. The danger with this program is that, as Nietzsche's aphorism expresses it, if you look into the abyss, the abyss eventually will look back into you. Betti had discovered and rediscovered the abyss through the introduction of foreigners, strangers, the friends of one's youth, or acquaintances unexpectedly returning, judges, inquirers, policemen, or characters turned into self-investigators by an unforgettable event claiming explanation or by a wish for atonement—as in *The Burnt Flower-Bed*—or an unusual, epiphanic circumstance—as in *The Queen and the Rebels*.

Now the abyss is staring back into the artist's soul. He doesn't have to look for it. There is no inquiry in *The Fugitive*; no event will bring to the fore a hidden layer of a character's life. It seems as if this play starts off, for the protagonist, where several others had finished. In the very first moments Betti peremptorily draws the audience's attention to what he wants to be the kernel of our interest. These are only a few moments, but they have the power and the intent to set everything that will happen afterwards in a particular interpretative direction: the stage is dark, a ray of light gradually becomes brighter; the protagonist, Nina, enters *"almost running, pursued in the dark by that ray, and by some kind of heavy footsteps."*[137] It is not a friendly light, not a light by which Nina will be able to walk and see better; she runs from it, she prefers darkness. But the ray cannot be avoided. It is as menacing as the footsteps. The play's first line seems to come from the pursuing ray. In an *"ironic and hostile"* tone it asks: "What are you doing here, Nina? Where are you going?... Why are you running away? What are you going to do? Nina. Nina. Nina."[138] Soon the stage is lit and the scene changes into a more realistic mode. Those first moments present a scene of common nightmare—of not being able to run fast enough to get away from something fearful. By itself it could be a playlet by Beckett, arational, suggestive, and which communicates on a level below consciousness. Within the context of the drama it epitomizes its meaning.

The play which follows is a reaction to the questioning voice. Nina would prefer not to face those questions, but they are always in her mind. The same voice will be heard by the audience in the second act, *"mocking and mellifluous"*: "Where will you go, Nina. What are you going to do?" To which she responds: "I'd like to escape, but I know it isn't possible."[139] The metaphor of the drama is: Once you have seen the abyss—of the inexistence of answers—then what? Then one may become mad and, like Nina, do things "without reason" and "out of place."

Betti presents Nina's madness with poignancy and delicacy. Her husband, Daniele, recounts her fate to a character called the Doctor: "I began to suspect it for the first time because of a...flower. Nina embroiders.... Well, one day it struck me that in every one of her patterns she introduced a flower, always the same one. There was no reason for it, and sometimes it was quite out of place...strange looking.... A sort of signature...The fact is that Nina's mad."[140] This description may seem sentimental, out of a second-rate "romantic" work, if it were not for the fact that it is pronounced toward the end of Act II, after we have been shown in stark and horrific terms the edge on which the heroine is standing. Another symptom of Nina's tormented soul is her special scream. Daniele tells us she utters it very often, and by the end of the first act we have heard it twice. "It is a cry...filled with terror."[141]

Of course, it is madness as metaphor, and, as if anticipating speculations of the late 1970's,[142] Betti takes the metaphor a little further; he wants to deny that it is a matter of so far undiscovered antipsychotic drugs. After learning that Nina is mad in the "technical sense," the Doctor, who is a doctor of chemistry, asserts that if that is so, then she is not responsible for anything, that the scream means nothing in particular. To which Daniele retorts: "No. An earthquake cracks open the land, but it certainly doesn't create scorpions. If scorpions come crawling out, it means they were there already."[143]

These are the scorpions coming out of the abyss. Nina communicates their presence with her continual screaming. The terror expressed by it in this play is not the same terror of the preceding plays — of the dark wood, of chaos, of lack of universal harmony, of justice, of inauthenticity. Nina's terror has no origin because there is nothing else. It is equated with life, in fact with light. Nina prefers darkness — most of Act I and the other two acts take place at night — and she "holds a grudge against the very air she breathes"[144] as well as "against her home and against everything else."[145] When Daniele asks why that is so, the Doctor, *"losing his patience"* answers: "that life itself is the biggest mistake of all, that life is the agent of your suffering."[146] The words remind us of Giacomo's remark in *Troubled Waters*:

"Perhaps it is the fact of existence itself which is dirty."[147] But Giacomo, like several other Bettian characters, speaks of having wasted his life or having lived the wrong life as if they could have experienced a different personal parabola, and their "play" could have had a different peripateia. Not so for Nina. No matter how changed her life would have been, nothing could have stopped her screaming. There is no parabola in her life; there is no peripateia in *The Fugitive*. In regard to Nina the play starts with the *lysis* (the lowest point of her life).

The play is constructed around three main characters: Nina, the sufferer; Daniele, the questioner; and the Doctor who not only denies the possibility of answers but argues the futility of questions. The story is quite simple. Nina has been playing cards with Giulio, her husband's direct superior. They are at the Naiad, the bar where they usually play. Nina has lost too big a sum for her to repay, and Giulio blackmails her; she has to give herself to him. Having sent Daniele to Bologna, Giulio will go to her home tonight. Nina, who cannot escape, consents.

But instead of going to Bologna, Daniele goes to a house in the mountains near the frontier where he had rented a room there weeks before. Here he meets the Doctor and confesses that he wants to cross the border. He has juggled the accounts a little and has debts, but the main reason for running away is that he "wasn't happy down there."[148] Most of all, he would like to get away from Nina, though now he is not so sure. The Doctor is a strange character, half-philosopher/half-devil, but a "modern" devil whose mode of temptation is not old-style passion. On the contrary, he preaches detachment, encouraging Daniele to cross the border, leaving everything and everyone behind.

In spite of his earlier decision, however, Daniele still feels attached to his wife; he cannot forget her horrid scream, her hatred for everything; he feels responsible for Nina, his alter ego. The Doctor, on the other hand, explains that he should feel free because "the whole business is just a...coincidence. Nothing inevitable in the fact that *you*—yes you—and that chair...exist together...Pure coincidence. Blind chance...Daniele by himself, the chair by itself and your wife...by herself. What...brought you together? The ludicrous paste of coincidence."[149] And the Doctor continues: If one doesn't believe in the "hypothesis" of pure co-incidence, then one must believe in order, in good and evil, based on the hypothesis of a "Primum Mobile." But this is also absurd because when God creates a human being, with all his weak-nesses and without his consent, He is in effect saying: "You are about to enter the world of existent things...which...can no longer not exist.... You are entering the world, where you have no escape, where you will find no place to hide."[150] For the Doctor there never has been a prelapsarian condition of exis-tence: creation started as an expulsion not from Eden but from the void, and it will end in the void or in hell—a reference to the lines on the door of Dante's Hell is clear.

Betti succeeds in giving coincidence and its alternate a theat-rical existence by placing these two scenes—the one at the bar with Nina and Giulio, the other in the mountains with Daniele and the Doctor—side by side on the stage. The pairs of char-acters interrupt one another's dialogues and seem, at times, to be speaking to one another despite the distance between them. That is another coincidence, like the Doctor's coincidences. In this play Betti also uses several other of his pet devices—a narrator, a chorus, as in *Troubled Waters*, the dead as in *Landslide* and *The Gambler*—almost a compendium of his stagecraft.

In Act II, Daniele, unconvinced by the devil's theories, goes back home: The Doctor understands that "one is always fasci-nated by the brink of the abyss."[151] Giulio having visited Nina, thinks she has given him deadly rat poison; frightened, he runs outside and faints in front of the house. To help Nina, Daniele, thinking him dead, dumps the body in a nearby lake to really drown. But they are discovered, and the devil-Doctor appears again urging Daniele to run away by himself. As they are about to be arrested, Daniele jumps onto a car taking Nina away with him. She is wounded by the police.

Act III takes place in the mountains. Daniele wants to save Nina by crossing the frontier. At this moment, first Giulio's mother and then Giulio's ghost appear and forgive them. But right after the "ironic" Doctor arrives. Daniele in desperation rails against God: "Why do you deny us everything? Why do you torment us, why do you exact so much from us? What is it you want?"[152] He cries at the absence of justice in the infliction of pain. But *"a new character"* has come into being: *"thunder*, reverberating through the mountains." This new character — a symbol of God — answers Daniele's outbursts of anger, but the Doctor again wants to convince Daniele that there is "nothing. (*He picks up a glowing piece of wood, and writes the word in the darkness*) N-O-T-H-I-N-G."[153] There isn't even someone to rebel against. Nina's last words — "Oh Daniele, why? Why did I weep! Why did I cry out?"[154] — are of utter despair. Daniele answers that she cried out "because someone was listening": he turns to the mountains and the *"thunder seems to answer him."* He asks the people around him to help him give Nina "a Christian burial," while the Doctor leaves muttering: "Fools! Blockheads! Idiots!"[155]

The play ends with the people carrying Nina's body off, singing a funeral chant to God. But Nina has screamed and tried to run away all her life. The abyss was there; if there is a God, the abyss is there in spite of Him. And the dirge of the believers can be based only on one of the mephistophelean Doctor's hypotheses. But Nina's damnation is owing neither to pure coincidence nor a primum mobile; it is a datum of destiny. She remains alone with her scream "expressing...pain...but also...a sense of terrible majesty."[156] Hers is the unjustifiable and unbearable suffering and majestic dignity projected at the end of their dramas by Oedipus, Cadmus, or King Lear.

The Fugitive reminds us of Greek and Shakespearean tragedy — it is a tragedy that "tells us that the spheres of reason, order, and justice are terribly limited"[157] and will not prevail. Betti's career as a dramatist seems somewhat to repeat the history of tragic theater as Gassner views it: It begins with the Greeks asking "How shall we exist?" and "after three thousand years of human effort to solve the first question," ends with another, Pirandello's "Do we exist at all?"[158] All his life Betti seems to have confronted the Socratic riddle, "How shall we live our life?" and in his last play seems to ask: "Is life worth living?" What remains is death which the very young Betti — in the last words of his doctoral dissertation — once described as life's "most democratic and stupidest event...."[159]

Part II. The Minor Works

Chapter 6

Poetry

I. Il re pensieroso

Betti's first literary work is a translation in delicate blank verse of the *Epithalamion of Thetis and Peleus* by Catullus, which Betti published at the end of his high school years, in 1910. He wrote his first original poems, however, as a prisoner of war in Germany in 1917 and 1918. These poems (revised) and other composed after the war were published in 1922 in his first book of poetry *Il re pensieroso* (*The Pensive King*). Then and now critics have discovered or thought to have discovered in these poems Betti's disparate sources, Italian and foreign: the school of the *crepuscolari*, Corazzini, Gozzano, Govoni, Pascoli, D'Annunzio, Maeterlinck, Andreyev, Poe, and the young Rilke.

Whether Betti is imitating directly—all critics note, for example, his imitation of Maeterlinck's *La mort de Tintagiles*— or merely remembering usable texts, the abundance of these texts points to the effort of the would-be artist *in fieri*. They have one thing in common: they refer to content not form, a clear sign that Betti was still seeking a personal voice. Although one critic thinks many of them are "clear stylistic exercises,"[1] some do express the sensitiveness of a man in search not just of style but of an understanding of the world of men and things seen (as it were) for the first time. In fact, according to one student of Betti the word that best would describe this collection is "enchantment."[2]

In rhythmic verse and imaginative language, which makes the physical ethereal and the unreal physical, Betti presents a melody[3] — at times broken and facile, but not always felicitous — a universe of magic and dream; a world seen through the innocent eye of a child. Yet it is not the pure and miraculous unreality of a child's fable, but that reality remembered by the adult.[4] Hence the melancholy, the nostalgia, the sense of precariousness, the unrealizable longing that suffuse the majority of the poems. Hence death, sickness, solitude, poverty. Some of the titles themselves are suggestive: *La casa morta* (*The Dead House*), *Il castello nero* (*The Black Castle*), *Le fanciulle povere* (*Poverty-stricken Girls*), *La principessa cieca* (*The Blind Princess*), *Le notti senza luna* (*Nights Without Moon*), and the title poem. The book represents a unfulfilled desire to escape from adult reality.

II. Canzonette — La morte

Betti's second volume of poetry, *Canzonette — La morte* (*Little Songs — Death*) collects verse written from 1922 to 1930; it received the poetry prize of the Accademia Mondadori in 1931, and it was published the following year. These poems convey different inspirational polarities which follow the intellectual and spiritual development of the author. Betti himself explains the contrast of the two-prong title: "*Canzonette*: an ingenuous, lively, enchanted joy of living. *La morte*: moments of silence and of solitude in which everything is distanced and what remains is only an obsessive fear of dying."[5]

The component of fable and dream-like fantasy now has a tone of tenuousness and an atmosphere of gentility which was missing from *The Pensive King*, in which Betti burdened his poems with allegorical meaning. *La fanciulla mutata in rio* (*The Girl Changed into a Brook*), and *Piccola nuvola di primavera* (*Small Spring Cloud*) are the most appealing of the collection for their musicality and litheness of touch.

The poems dealing directly with life and death show a Betti

nearer the playwright, who by now (1929) has already composed
The Mistress of the House, The House on the Water, and *An Inn
on the Harbor* which depict pain, sickness, solitude, cruelty, and
death. In these poems the sweet melancholy of the fable becomes
bitterness at the contemplation of man condemned to toil within
a heartless social setting and an indifferent nature. The critic
Adriano Tilgher praises in them Betti's "desperate sincerity...
courageous denunciation of all conventional lies,...nakedness, and
virility."[6] Another critic Emilio Barbetti, describes their language
as "extraordinarily bodily..., smelling...of blood and sweat."[7]

Some revealing titles are *La giornata dell'uomo* (*Man's Day*),
two *Canto di emigranti* (*Emigrants' Song*), *Peccato originale*
(*Original Sin*), *Canzonetta del peccatore senza conforto* (*Little
Song of the Sinner Without Comfort*), and *Canto di operai*
(*Workers' Song*), in which a part of the protagonists' prayer
reads:

> La morte, vedemmo, la morte,
> su noi, sui figli, da tutte le porte,
> nei ventri pregni, su ogni sorte,
> la morte, la morte,
> sul grande stento senza frutto,
> sopra la luce, sopra tutto.
> ...
> ....rispondi!
> Accendi per noi la stella senza tramonti![8]

> (Death, we saw death,
> Over us, over our children, through all the doors,
> In pregnant wombs, over each destiny,
> Death, death
> Over our great fruitless hardship,
> Over the light, over everything.
> ...
> ....answer!
> Light for us the never setting star.)

The poem ends with the line: "A dark wind carried off the shout-
ing!"[9] The uncoordination between the accumulation of images

and their rhythm prevents the success of the poem. Betti's commitment — though sincere — is filtered through literariness. In this and many other poems there is purpose but not that "purposiveness without purpose" Kant thought necessary to art.

III. Uomo e donna

Unomo e donna (1937; *Man and Woman*), Betti's third book of poetry, gathers the poems of 1932 to 1934. Some of its verse is the closest Betti came to pure poetical expression. One critic, Liliana Luzzani, speaks, in regard to some of these poems, of the poet's "highest moments."[10] Betti abandons the bitterness of his past poetry; he conveys a resigned acceptance of man's lot in the universe; he abandons the fables and the dreams which attracted him before.

He sings now of creation, the history of the universe and of man. His intention is to compose a kind of grandiose epic poetry, and the poems are connected by an underlying conceptual thread, evident in the titles of the four parts into which the book is divided. The first is *La terra* (*The Earth*), where the author contemplates the miracle of the birth of life slowly appearing on the crust of the earth, and the coming of man into the universe. It ends, in the last poem, with an apocalyptic vision of suffering humanity: "copriva / un brulichio di vecchi e storpi la terra."[11] ("The earth was covered by a teeming of old and crippled people.") The second part, *Vincere la morte* (*To Conquer Death*) is a rebellion against such destiny; it sings of hope in the immortality of man. The third part, whose title is the book's title, contains the most touching pages of Betti's verse, and also the most controversial. Some of the former are those which depict the first embrace of the first man and woman. Betti had written of this embrace in his preceding book with a feeling of sadness *post coitum*: "Su ogni donna, stesa e nuda, / s'avviticchia un moribondo" ("On top of every woman, stretched out and naked, clings a moribund man").[12] Now in the poem which gives the title to the third part and to the book, Betti writes of "...quella letizia/ quel caldo d'infanzia, di tenere foglie"; ("...that joy / that warmth of infancy, of tender leaves";). There remains a sense of delicacy not sadness: "Udendo a lui il cuore / martellare come a un morente/ ella, leggera, gli carezzava i capelli" ("Hearing his heart beating like a dying man's, she, light, caressed his hair").[13]

Betti's less pessimistic view of man's destiny also carries a socio-political optimism, a belief in the brotherhood of human beings. Perhaps aided, or blinded, by an "apparently lasting political and religious relaxation," which Fascism inspired at the beginning of the 1930's soon after the Patti Lateranensi (1929),[14] Betti trusts to the Italian political situation of the time. He writes the poem *I Capi* (*The Leaders*) in which he speaks of "One... above the crowd" who can bring unity and dignity.

In the fourth and last part, *Gli angeli* (*The Angels*), Betti sings of death as the moment when man will enter the bliss of afterlife

> là dove non è più ombra, luggiù
> sovra i prati di splendido colore
> là vanno e vengono le migliaia e le migliaia
> là sono le leggiadre pensierose creature
> venute da mondi spenti.[15]
>
> (There where there is no shadow, over there
> In the meadows of splendid color
> There come and go thousands and thousands,
> There are the graceful pensive creatures
> Come from extinguished worlds.)

IV. Ultime liriche (1938–1953)

Most of the poems Betti composed after 1935 were published posthumously in 1957 as *Ultime liriche (1938-1953)* [*Last Lyrics (1938-1953)*]. Here one finds the most autobiographical aspects of Betti's poetry. He remembers nostalgically the region of his childhood and youth; he writes of family affection now gone forever. In these poems Betti seems to forget himself and to achieve a momentary sense of peace and joy.

Although a small selection of his verse raises itself above the level of versification, Betti's poetry must be considered among his minor work—a very minor contribution to Italian twentieth century poetry and outside its mainstream whose major figures are Campana, Saba, Quasimodo, Ungaretti, and Montale.

Chapter 7

Prose

I. Caino

As he was finishing his first book of poetry, Betti began writing his first short stories, some of which appeared in Italian newspapers in and outside of Italy. Betti collected thirteen of these stories and five fables – all written between 1919 and 1924 – and published them in 1928 under the title *Caino*.

The most interesting of these fables is *La verità* ("The Truth"), both for its incisiveness and for the influence of Pirandello. Besides the obvious fact that the title repeats one of Pirandello's, Betti also deals in it with the relativism of truth, Pirandello's intellectual mode. Betti's protagonist, however, is merely emotionally undone at the disappointment he experiences on discovering the absence of an absolute. He doesn't reach the sphere of metaphysical questioning and "doesn't discover the abyss of nothingness."[1] Pirandello ends his story with the impossibility of ever knowing one's real self, Betti ends his fable with a psychoanalytical insight. The Pirandellian protagonist cannot return to life as it was before his truth is revealed: he has to go to jail. Betti's protagonist would like to reject a life forever "without joy," as that "knowing Jew" – an allusion to Freud? – calls it, but it is impossible; for "when [truth] has made its sneer felt once, there isn't a way to silence it any longer."[2]

133

The same interests Betti displayed in his poetry are also present in *Caino*, especially in the fables, two of which in particular reproduce "the sentiments and stylistical attitudes"[3] of the protagonists of the poetry collection *The Pensive King: Il principe Desiderio* ("Prince Desire") and *Il principe che teme di morire* ("The Prince Afraid to Die"). In the first a prince searches for happiness, just as King Nadir does in the drama *The Marvelous Island*. He meets an innocent and beautiful young girl, with "sincere eyes, in which he feels trust, peace, sweetness."[4] But after he has enjoyed her, that "marvelous toy,"[5] he looks at her with hate. She kills herself and the prince returns to his desperate search.

In the second fable, "The Prince Afraid to Die," a king shelters his son from the knowledge of death. But when his son discovers death, he runs away from the palace in search of a reason for existence, meaningless because it must end.

Although Betti constructs the short stories in this collection in realistic detail, some of the elements of fable remain. The stories usually possess allegorical meaning which is sometimes too apparent, and some of the situations are extraordinary and extreme. Furthermore, there is an underlying sentimentality in many of them which implies superficiality if not insincerity.

La cancellata ("The Gate") is typical: a hungry beggar attracted by a piece of bread meets a lonely child who is standing at the iron gate of a garden. The beggar who today is by chance and charity well dressed tries to soothe the child's melancholy. He invents for him a tale of his very beautiful beloved who lives in a palace full of mirrors and velvet. At the end the child gives the bread to another beggar.

The most original story in the collection and the most intense—it is only four pages—is *Viaggio notturno* ("Night Trip"). Sitting in a darkened bus, an unhappy and hopeless man is "content that it is dark, as if his true face is able to unmask itself only in darkness."[6] On considering his unlucky lot, he doesn't know whether to laugh or cry. He feels cold, and he is angry. Suddenly he senses "pressed strongly against his hand the soft and mysterious weight of a woman's thigh."[7] He starts touching the inside of her thighs, angry and disdainful of her silent willingness. "He whispers, panting: 'Bitch! Bitch!'...That docility frightens and infuriates him."[8] But when suddenly her hand "timidly" touches his "as if to be forgiven," he realizes she is just like himself, another sad creature who in the dark is able to overcome her shame and to caress his hand, anybody's hand. His anger changes into pity. They pass the rest of the trip together holding hands. When she gets off the bus, they have not exchanged a word or seen each other's face.

In "Night Trip," darkness allows men to shed their masks and frees them to see themselves in their vulnerability; it allows them to express their longing for fraternity. In the story "Caino," however, Betti presents for the first time and in convincing language the realization that evil and sorrow are part of life and that no amount of hope can relieve the anguish of human existence. At the beginning we learn that the protagonist is marked by God. Just so, no reasons. The people with whom he is in contact, including his mother, seem to participate in God's gratuitous wrath toward him. He is pushed further and further into shame and self-hatred, and into hatred for his gentle, beautiful, enviable and envied brother whom he kills. In "Night Trip" and "Caino" Betti "happily succeeds in mixing [a] desire for life with a painful sense of it."[9]

II. Le case

Instead of entitling his second book of stories after one of the stories in it, Betti took his title from the *Little Songs — Death*: the poem *Le case* (*Houses*) expressed his despair at the meaninglessness of men and things: "vuoto è lo spazio nero. / Fugge in esso... / ...la terra tonda. // S'alzano s'alzano case quadrate.// In ogni casa, come in un orto, / ogni tanto matura un morto."[10] ("Space is empty, black. In it the round earth turns. Square houses rise and rise. In every house, as in a vegetable garden, once in a while a dead man ripens.") The same gloomy vision is operative in the stories of this volume, and, in this sense, the book is unified: the stories are obsessive expressions of the same fixation: Why life, if it equals suffering?

Betti usually makes the community his protagonist in these

stories, and even in those that focus on one character, the center of the story is not the presentation of the single person but — with the exception of *Incidente al 4° Km* — the way he is enveloped by the "others" who also experience his predicament and whose lives he cannot help sharing. The apartments symbolize the pettiness and restriction of life which excludes privacy and individuality; the inhabitants of them can hear each other beyond their walls. When Betti takes the reader into offices, tribunals, and hospitals, life proves not very different.

Una giornata ("A Day") is one of the most representative of these stories. Betti himself has spoken of his desire to reproduce a "manner of narrative almost cinematographic."[11] He starts with a long shot of a tenement, zooms into the interior of an apartment, and then focuses on Massimo, the man whose day is going to be the subject of his narration. Betti follows his protagonist from bed in the morning to bed at night. His day is full of small, stupid occupations, routines not only without excitement but also without the most elementary joy, affection, or satisfaction. His first worry at dawn, the dripping faucet, will also be one of his last before going to sleep. Both at work and at home the main topic of concern is the rising price of cooking gas. To Massimo all the people coming and going, from home to work, from work to home, and then again the same after midday dinner "seem an agonizing thing,...comic."[12] Domesticity repels him, yet, before falling asleep he starts copulating with his wife lovelessly, almost passionlessly.

A similar hopelessness, daily and silent, appears in the other stories as well. At times the atmosphere may remind the reader of some of Chekhov's pages, although Betti's narration often loses its magic by the repeated introduction of extraneous detail. Betti emphasizes a tragedy of nonevents, of uselessness: the stories are based on "states of feeling which slowly determine a situation."[13] In fact, the actions that take place become indicative and poignant for their flatness and the flatness of the lives in which they occur. The stories *Quelli del terzo* ("Those on the Third") and *Mezzanino, l'uscio a destra* ("Mezzanine, the Door to the Right") are two good examples. In the first a couple living in an apartment fight every evening when the husband comes from work.

They fight (apparently) about the most trivial things—today because of the cabbage smell—but the real reason for their anger is life itself: "both of them claim it desperately, their life, their life ruined, finished."[14] So while they scream at each other, some neighbors, knowing that their argument is not such an exceptional event but part of an unavoidable suffering, take care lest supper be burnt. After all, "at a certain moment it will be necessary indeed to swallow it, this supper."[15]

Although the furtive lovemaking of "Mezzanine, the Door to the Right" is consummated in the dark and hidden from everybody's knowledge, the neighbors can be heard "in the small courtyard, in the balconies, as they cough, move, cook, and flush the bathroom water."[16] The banality of the surrounding, the stupid, everyday noises deny the lovers the specialness of their moment of passion. "It seemed unlikely to her, now, that the day after she would have boiled milk again. Since the day after she could also have killed herself, or gone for a walk, or darned the linen, everything was the same."[17] The bleakness of the surroundings makes them realize the bleakness of their own situation, and when they start making love, each of them feels pity for himself and the other.

The protagonist of *Incidente al 4° Km* ("Accident at the Fourth Km") is the most sharply profiled figure in the book. A young boy throws himself onto the railroad tracks because he is "an angel, too noble, shy," forcing the station clerk to think of himself as the pure boy he once was. The ghost of that pure boy now accuses the clerk of having betrayed him. At the boy's funeral, as if he himself were in the casket, the man asks the boy's "forgiveness, for something delicate, precious, that was betrayed, ruined forever."[18] The only escape from the brutality of living is not living.

The book's last story, *I poveri* ("The Poor") records a surreal and apocalyptic procession of the sick, the old, the poor, and the weak. They advance endlessly like a "black sea" as if to reach a "rainbow." The vision is broken by what seems to be an attack, veiled and perhaps not completely conscious on Fascism's self-attributed grandeur: "It seemed almost grotesque, while watching all this [the procession], that there existed big monuments

with gold statues, battleships in ports shooting blanks, cere-
monies with brass bands, crowds in tuxedos on red carpets, law-
yers' speeches in parliaments.... They seemed macabre jokes...
while there were people who were about to die and people who
were already dying."[19]

III. Una strana serata

Betti's third and last volume of short stories came out in
1948. All of the stories had been published in various magazines
and newspapers, some ten years before, and a few, as Di Pietro
speculates,[20] had perhaps been written even earlier, at the time he
was composing the stories and fables of *Houses*. Indeed, half a
dozen of the stories in *Una strana serata* (*A Strange Evening*)
could have been part of the preceding book. In *Notte al commis-
sariato* ("Night at the Inspector's Office"), for example, the main
characters are a man and a wife who fight every evening for no
special reason just as a similar couple fight every evening in
"Those on the Third" from *Houses*. Similarly the protagonist of
Signore anziano prima di cena ("Old Gentleman Before Dinner")
finds himself in the same predicament as the protagonist of "A
Day." Each feels the uselessness of his daily routine, and each
thinks of his family without joy. The old gentleman looks at his
wife (who is very pleasant) and cannot help thinking that his life
has been a "secret waiting" for a "marvelous immense love [which
now] is too late," and so he asks himself: "What was the use of all
this bustling around?"[21]

The other stories of *A Strange Evening* do not recall their
predecessors. They are all characterized by a nostalgic remembrance for the places and people of the author's childhood and
youth. The plots and the protagonists are only "pretexts"[22] to
capture old sights, images, sounds, voices, and to relive them
once more. In consequence, each story is recounted in the first
person, although Betti's tone is never carefree. He doesn't forget
himself but continuously infuses these pages with an awareness
that what he remembers is not only past but also—and this aspect
gives the stories their special poignancy—that it has never been

happy. For instance, Betti rarely depicts his narrator in thought-less play with his childhood friends. In *I giuocatori* ("The Players") the relation between the two boys playing cards in the barns is not one of affection but of envy and power, just as among the adults in the farm village. The story ends with the narrator describing one of the boys, the sensitive and superior one, as "almost happy."[23]

Il tempo fuggito ("Time Run Away") begins as the happy re-membrance of a seventeen year old boy kissing an older girl who once had held him in her arms as a very small child; now she coyly lets herself be kissed. But Betti cannot leave this idyll without a gloomy frame. After leaving the girl, the boy goes to a cemetery to place a bunch of wild flowers on the tomb of a six year old girl, and the story ends with the narrator sighing about those beautiful mornings of his youth: "How is it possible that everything [those mornings] disappeared?... It seems incredible to me; yet something, in my heart, hopes it is not true."[24]

In *La casa solitaria* ("The Solitary House") the author re-treats a step further in time and recalls not his own childhood memories but his grandmother's. He retells her tale of how her own father lived on and alone after his wife died giving birth to the narrator's grandmother, and how her ghost seems to have prevented him from killing his daughter accidently.

Perhaps the story where sentimentality most visibly becomes anguish is *Il viso della donna morta* ("The Dead Woman's Face"). The narrator introduces here not a memory but the forgetting of one. The protagonist is a guest of Gemma's parents, his long-dead love, and he discovers that, to his surprise, it requires "a certain effort, a kind of concentration," to remember her face. He is also amazed that while he is trying to think of her, "other and indifferent faces—that of a certain Mrs. Santoni...or of the seamstress, two faces that, after all, *don't* resemble at all *his* beloved's"[25]—cancel out her image. But at the end, after failing to remember her face, the narrator feels relaxed "as if for a long time *he* had held up a weight and that now *he* had let it go."[26] If this ironic insight, that longed-for memories may be a burden in that they prevent a fuller experience of the present, were more visible, these stories of reminiscence would be more compelling.

Beyond those stories in the manner of *Houses* and those based on memories of childhood, there is a third kind of narrative exemplified by the title story, which is the first and longest of the book. In it a young man visits the director of a big company evidently to intercede on behalf of a suspended employee. Or so the director supposes as he delivers a harangue about duty and responsibility. But his visitor merely smiles and nods, and when the director stops, explains that he hasn't come into the office to complain but to escape the cold. This odd event sets the quasi-surreal tone of the text. In "A Strange Evening" Betti passes easily from the realistic to the dream-like to the unreal itself, unifying them as he goes and suggesting the surreality of everyday life.

IV. La piera alta

Betti elaborated his only novel *La piera alta* (*The High Stone*), which he published in 1948, from his movie script, *I tre del Pra' di Sopra* (*The Three Men from the Meadow*). He wrote it while composing the plays *The Inquiry*, *Crime on Goat Island*, and *Struggle Till Dawn* and some of the short stories of reminiscence which he published in the collection *A Strange Evening*. The novel in fact preserves two separate tones: one reminds us of those stories in the joys, troubles, and ideals of the child's life, while the other depicts the adult struggle to find oneself and to make human contact with the "others." This second part is connected with the pessimism of the plays Betti was then writing.

The novel begins as ten year old Guido—on summer vacation in a mountain village—meets two other boys, Rigo and Marcone, and a girl, Giovannina. This village is near the top of a mountain, the High Stone, one side of which no one has ever been able to climb. To climb it—as Rigo says three times—"is the most difficult thing in the world."[27] The boys attempt the mountain surreptitiously, Guido participating in spite of his fear, but they remain stuck on an edge and cannot come back. In the evening, Giovannina, who knows their plan, tells the villagers who rescue the boys.

Notwithstanding Guido's cowardice — he untied himself from the rope which bound them — Rigo and Marcone feel a bond of friendship for him, whereas Guido feels contempt for their coarseness. Yet he senses they are more sincere and kind than he is, and he is overwhelmed by the "disheartening thought that *he* would never be like them."[28] The boys meet again for several more summers, then lose sight of each other.

In the second part of the novel Guido, now an engineer, is sent by his company to supervise a mine excavation in a mountain village; he is about to refuse the assignment, but when he discovers it is the village of his youthful experiences, he eagerly accepts, as if to test himself again and start his life anew.

In fact, he has always been obsessed by "that worry of *his* youth, that impression of climbing toward strange and dangerous places high above the rest of the world."[29] And, in fact, he is still unable to give shape to his life. In the new events of his life he is still "unable to see...a thread. Everything seems futile, guided by nothing but stupefied and stupid chance."[30] He is incapable of communicating with others: he senses that "between *himself* and them there had always been a kind of secret, maybe things which they had not told *him* or asked of *him*, and which *he* had not told or asked of them."[31] By the end of the book he has contributed indirectly to the accident which takes Rigo's life, and directly caused Marcone's unhappiness by taking away Giovanna, his fiancée, who has secretly loved Guido since she was Giovannina. Then he leaves her, and by the time he repents of his error, it is too late: she has run away from the village. Alone and lonely, he continues to look obsessively for her in every woman's face as if only she can deliver him from his destiny and give him the opportunity of a new life. Finally he realizes he has lost her forever. Near the end of the novel, he broods that "in the immense dark eternity there existed a chance and now [that] it is lost, now there will be immense dark and empty eternity."[32]

Betti succeeds in giving a more valid shape to several of the obsessions and interests of the novel in his theater. Here they are somewhat dispersed and (despite some wonderful pages) are at times totally forgotten in the welter of realistic detail.

V. Essays

Il diritto e la rivoluzione (*Law and Revolution*) is the title of the doctoral dissertation Betti wrote in the spring of 1914. It is useful for discovering the author's concerns — Marx, Nietzsche, D'Annunzio, Sorel, Max Stirner — and it may throw some light on the future playwright, but it is not essential for a better understanding of his creative work. If not an original work of philosophy, politics, or jurisprudence, Betti's dissertation is a lively argument which is based on the "common sense" premise that might makes right and that societal institutions are the expression of the stronger men of the moment. Successful revolutions destroy previously lawful entities and impose a new order; a new group of people takes command of society. But the final revolution — after which men "will be instinctive, well balanced, and compact like diamonds"[33] — will be against "concepts" like law, sin, criticism, and analysis; and the Nietzsche's ideal Apollonian man will triumph.[34] For "reform — Betti argues — is the masturbation of revolutionary force."[35]

In 1920 Betti published a treatise entitled *Considerazioni sulla forza maggiore come limite di responsabilità del vettore ferroviario* (*Consideration of Acts of God Limiting the Responsibility of Railroads*). Betti wrote it in order to become a legal consultant to the State Railroad. Contrary to the destructive spirit of the group which dominates his doctoral dissertation, Betti now takes pains to assign responsibility and guilt to the individual who should do well what he is supposed to do. This essay is of interest to the student of Betti because it is part of the background of his important play, *Landslide.*

Il canto XXIX del Paradiso is a lecture Betti gave in Rome on March 11, 1934, and which was published posthumously in 1957. In this canto Beatrice explains the creation and the angels to Dante, and Betti is particularly interested in the first willful act of the rebellious angels. He is attracted by the question of how it is possible for man to be guilty if God created him as he is. Betti answers that beyond free will there is a grace but that something in man must freely receive it.

Religione e teatro (*Religion and the Theater*) is another lecture Betti wrote in January 1953, also published in 1957. At this point of his life, a few months before his death, Betti had become a very devout Christian and in this lecture he is more interested in the question of good and evil than he is in theater. However, he presents some suggestive comments and insights on religious theater. He is convinced that "in error not all is error"[36]; and that "just as the grain of wheat presupposes the earth, and the fish, the water, man presupposes God."[37] He uses similar words at the end of his last play, *The Fugitive*. This lecture helps explain Betti's poetics more than his artistic achievements.

Chapter 8

Conclusion

Drama is the formal embodiment of crisis
(George Steiner, The Death of Tragedy*).*

With Western man in the twentieth century Betti shared a life of quiet despair, a sense of isolation, a condemnation to finitude, an urge to investigate, and an aspiration to otherness. With some twentieth century men he tried to express this condition of discontent. With a few he felt a continuum of crises from which man could be delivered by the expressivity of artistic form. With a very few he chose the theater as his medium of composition. With some of his plays he achieves suspensions of discontent which momentarily exorcise the ugliness of crisis but which do not deliver us from the feeling of inevitable apocalypse. This openness of vision allows the plays to remain rediscoverable, capable of transporting man from the profane to the sacred.

Betti didn't belong to a school, and although the distinguished dramatist Diego Fabbri uses the Bettian form of inquest in his plays, Betti didn't set any Bettian trend. Together with Fabbri, Eduardo De Filippo, Dario Fo, and a few others he represents modern Italian theater. When critics wrote that Betti is the best modern Italian playwright after Pirandello, the specification was ambiguous, pointing to time and implying achievement. Betti is Betti; his best is incomparable.

144

Notes

Preface

1. Auden, W.H., "Postscript: Christianity an Art," in *Selected Essays* (London, 1962), p. 216.
2. Ugo Betti, "Religion and the Theatre," trans. by Gino Rizzo and William Meriwether, *The Tulane Drama Review*, V, 2 (1960), p. 12.
3. Ugo Betti, "Preface to *The Mistress*," *Ibid.*, p. 13.
4. E. Martin Browne, Introduction to *Three European Plays* (London, 1965), p. 9.

Chapter 1

1. Antonio Di Pietro characterizes it as "left fascist." *L'opera di Ugo Betti* (Bari, 1968), I, 80.
2. Among the *rondisti* there were Cardarelli, Cecchi, Bacchelli, Savinio, Barilli, and Falqui. *Ibid.*, p. 78.
3. Henry Reed, Foreword to *Three Plays by Ugo Betti*, trans. by H. Reed. (New York, 1958), p. 7.

Chapter 2

1. Ugo Betti, *Teatro completo* (Bologna, 1971), p. 26. Translations are mine unless otherwise stated.
2. *Ibid.*, p. 27.

3. *Ibid.*, p. 45.
4. *Ibid.*, p. 50.
5. *Ibid.*, p. 46.
6. *Ibid.*, p. 27.
7. *Ibid.*, p. 31.
8. *Ibid.*
9. *Ibid.*, p. 44.
10. *Ibid.*, p. 46.
11. *Ibid.*, p. 59.
12. *Ibid.*, p. 50.
13. Gildo Moro, *Il teatro di Ugo Betti* (Milan, 1973), pp. 13–14.
14. Betti, *Teatro completo*, p. 65.
15. *Ibid.*
16. *Ibid.*, p. 66.
17. *Ibid.*, p. 70.
18. *Ibid.*
19. *Ibid.*, p. 80.
20. *Ibid.*, p. 81.
21. *Ibid.*, p. 87.
22. *Ibid.*, p. 96.
23. *Ibid.*
24. *Ibid.*, p. 97.
25. *Ibid.*
26. *Ibid.*, p. 101.
27. François de Malherbe, *Consolation à M. Du Périer, Oeuvres poétiques* (Paris, 1968), p. 158. For *Fioretti*, Rilke and Foscolo, *Teatro completo*, pp. 104, 109, 116.
28. Betti, *Teatro completo*, p. 104.
29. *Ibid.*
30. *Ibid.*, p. 110.
31. *Ibid.*, p. 125.
32. *Ibid.*, p. 137.
33. Betti, "Religion and the Theatre," pp. 11–12.
34. Cioacchino Pellecchia, *Saggio su Ugo Betti* (Naples, 1963), p. 51.
35. G.B. De Sanctis, "Senso della crisi in Ugo Betti," *Studi sul teatro* (Ravenna, 1968), p. 227.
36. C. Bruner, "La condizione umana di Ugo Betti," *Studium*, LVI, 11 (1960), p. 759.
37. Vito Pandolfi, "Italian Theatre Since the War," *The Tulane Drama Review*, VII, 3 (1964), p. 92.
38. Betti, see Franco Cologni, *Ugo Betti* (Bologna, 1960), p. 35.

39. Di Pietro, II, 11, n. 2.

40. Pellecchia, p. 55.

41. Di Pietro, II, 14, n. 1.

42. Betti, *Teatro completo*, p. 182.

43. Moro, p. 52.

44. It has been observed that this tenderness echoes Betti's letters to his wife-to-be, Andreina. Di Pietro, II, 17, n. 2.

45. Baldo Curato, *Sessant'anni di teatro in Italia* (Milan, 1947), p. 332.

46. Betti, *Landslide* in *Three Plays on Justice*, trans. by G.H. McWilliam (San Francisco, 1964), p. 4. An Italian version of this reading of *Landslide* appeared in Emanuele Licastro, "Deragliamenti in *Frana allo Scalo Nord*," *NEMLA Italian Studies*, V (1981).

47. Emilio Barbetti, *Il teatro di Ugo Betti* (Florence, 1943), pp. 62–63.

48. Betti, *Landslide*, p. 4.

49. *Ibid.*, p. 11.

50. *Ibid.*, p. 7.

51. *Ibid.*, p. 21.

52. *Ibid.*

53. *Ibid.*, p. 24.

54. *Ibid.*, p. 34.

55. *Ibid.*, p. 30.

56. *Ibid.*, p. 40.

57. *Ibid.*, p. 43.

58. *Ibid.*, p. 47.

59. *Ibid.*, p. 48.

60. Of course, the victimized clerk has a long literary tradition: Gogol, Melville, Dostoyevsky, Pirandello.

61. Moro, p. 58.

62. Betti, *Landslide*, p. 45.

63. *Ibid.*, p. 44.

64. *Ibid.*, p. 55.

65. *Ibid.*, p. 56. In the words of Camus: "The certainty of a God giving a meaning to life far surpasses in attractiveness the ability to behave badly with impunity." *The Myth of Sisyphus* (New York, 1964), p. 67.

66. Betti, *Landslide*, p. 45.

67. Diego Fabbri considers the realistic beginning of *Landslide* a fault. In Achille Fiocco, *Ugo Betti* (Rome, 1954), p. 20.

68. Di Pietro, II, 58.

69. G.H. McWilliam, Introd. to *Three Plays on Justice, cit.*, p. xi.

70. Barbetti, pp. 77–78.

71. *Ibid.*, p. 83.

72. Betti, *Teatro completo*, p. 209.

73. Betti, *Landslide*, p. 42.

74. *Aristotle's Poetics.* Translation and Analysis by Kenneth A. Telford (Chicago, 1965), p. 53.

75. Barbetti, p. 89.

76. Betti, "Religion and the Theatre," p. 11.

77. Albert Camus, Introduction to the English translation of *The Myth of Sisyphus and Other Essays* (New York, 1964), p. v.

78. Paul Klee, "On Modern Art," in *Modern Artists on Art*, ed. by Robert L. Herbert (Englewood Cliffs, N.J., 1964), p. 87.

79. Betti, *Teatro completo*, p. 311.

80. Diego Fabbri, in Cologni, *Ugo Betti, cit.*, p. 51.

81. Betti, *Teatro completo*, p. 292.

82. *Ibid.*, p. 296.

83. *Ibid.*, p. 306.

84. *Ibid.*, p. 311.

85. *Ibid.*, p. 312.

86. *Ibid.*

87. *Ibid.*, p. 315.

88. Barbetti, p. 121.

89. Moro, p. 61.

90. Leonida Repaci, in Curato, *Sessant'anni di teatro in Italia, cit.*, p. 345.

91. Curato, p. 341.

92. Betti, *Teatro completo*, p. 320.

93. *Ibid.*, p. 322.

94. *Ibid.*

95. *Ibid.*

96. *Ibid.*, p. 292.

97. *Ibid.*, p. 293.

98. *Ibid.*

99. *Ibid.*

100. *Ibid.*, p. 313.

101. *Ibid.*, p. 293.

102. *Ibid.*

103. *Ibid.*

104. *Ibid.*

105. *Ibid.*, p. 320.

106. *Ibid.*, p. 326.

107. *Ibid.*

108. *Ibid.*, p. 398.
109. *Ibid.*, pp. 301–302.
110. *Ibid.*, p. 294.
111. *Ibid.*, p. 308.
112. *Ibid.*, p. 302.
113. *Ibid.*, p. 325.
114. *Ibid.*, p. 328.
115. Di Pietro, II, 129.
116. Sergio Torresani, *Il teatro italiano negli ultimi vent'anni (1945–1965)* (Cremona, 1965), p. 74.
117. Barbetti, p. 148.

Chapter 3

1. Betti, *Teatro completo*, p. 338.
2. Di Pietro, II, 30, n. 1.
3. Cologni, p. 62.
4. Betti, *Teatro completo*, p. 355.
5. *Ibid.*, p. 357.
6. *Ibid.*, p. 373.
7. Barbetti, p. 114.
8. G.H. McWilliam, "The Minor Works of Ugo Betti," *Italian Studies*, XX (1965), p. 85.
9. Betti, in an introductory note to this drama's first edition. *Il Dramma*, XIX, 397–8 (1943), p. 10.
10. Diego Fabbri, in Barbetti, *Il teatro di Ugo Betti, cit.*, p. 107.
11. Barbetti, pp. 107 and 116.
12. Di Pietro, II, 27.
13. McWilliam, p. 83.
14. Barbetti, p. 111.
15. Di Pietro, II, 29.
16. McWilliam, p. 87.
17. Betti, *Teatro completo*, p. 341.
18. McWilliam, p. 87.
19. Barbetti, p. 116.
20. Betti, *Teatro completo*, p. 343.
21. *Ibid.*, p. 342.
22. Søren Kierkegaard, *The Concept of Dread* (Princeton, 1957), p. 26.
23. Ernest Becker, *The Denial of Death* (New York, 1973), p. 26.
24. Betti, *Teatro completo*, pp. 337–338.

25. *Ibid.*, p. 362.

26. *Ibid.*, p. 364.

27. *Ibid.*, p. 341.

28. Becker, p. 32.

29. Barbetti, p. 110.

30. Cologni, pp. 63–64.

31. *Ibid.*, p. 60.

32. See Cologni, p. 64.

33. McWilliam, p. 79, n. 3.

34. *Ibid.*, p. 79.

35. Di Pietro, II, 137.

36. *Ibid.*, p. 129.

37. Ernst Kris, *Psychoanalytic Explorations in Art* (New York, 1952), p. 188.

38. *Ibid.*, p. 187.

39. *Ibid.*, p. 137, n. 4.

40. Betti, *Teatro completo*, p. 241.

41. *Ibid.*, p. 258.

42. *Ibid.*, p. 275.

43. Barbetti, p. 147.

44. Betti, in a note published in *Film* (8/7/39). Quoted by McWilliam, p. 89.

45. McWilliam, p. 100.

46. Di Pietro, II, 136.

47. Barbetti, p. 161, n. 338.

48. *Ibid.*

49. McWilliam, p. 100.

50. Betti, *Teatro completo*, p. 380.

51. Renato Simoni, *Corriere della Sera* (Milan, Feb. 21, 1942). Quoted by Cologni, *cit.*, p. 72.

52. Cologni, p. 69.

53. Betti, *Teatro completo*, p. 462.

54. *Ibid.*, p. 463.

55. *Ibid.*, p. 468.

56. *Ibid.*, p. 476.

57. *Ibid.*, p. 479.

58. *Ibid.*, p. 475.

59. *Ibid.*, p. 480.

60. *Ibid.*, p. 758.

61. *Ibid.*, pp. 770–771.

62. Moro, p. 136.

63. Betti, *Teatro completo*, p. 779.

64. *Ibid.*, p. 793.
65. McWilliam, p. 104.

Chapter 4

1. Betti, *Teatro completo*, p. 487.
2. R.D. Laing, *The Divided Self* (Baltimore, 1970), p. 87.
3. Betti, *Teatro completo*, p. 487.
4. *Ibid.*
5. Martin Heidegger, *Being and Time* (New York, 1962), p. 283.
6. Betti, *Teatro completo*, p. 489.
7. *Ibid.*, p. 492.
8. *Ibid.*
9. *Ibid.*, pp. 488 and 489.
10. Moro, p. 64.
11. Betti, *Teatro completo*, pp. 494–495.
12. *Ibid.*, p. 510.
13. *Ibid.*, p. 512.
14. *Ibid.*
15. Di Pietro, II, 150.
16. Betti, *Teatro completo*, p. 587.
17. Di Pietro, II, 176.
18. Betti, *Teatro completo*, p. 614.
19. *Ibid.*, p. 615.
20. *Ibid.*
21. Pellecchia, p. 76.
22. *Ibid.*
23. Betti, *Teatro completo*, p. 620.
24. *Ibid.*, p. 622.
25. De Sanctis, "Betti tra favola e realismo," in *Studi sul teatro, cit.*, p. 243. For a discussion on the importance of childhood memory in Betti, see Gino Rizzo, "Regression-Progression in Ugo Betti's Drama," *The Tulane Drama Review*, VIII (1963).
26. Betti, *Teatro completo*, p. 633.
27. Torresani, p. 77.
28. *Ibid.*, p. 78.
29. De Sanctis, p. 249.
30. Ruggero Jacobbi, "Ugo Betti nel paese degli angeli," in *Teatro di ieri e di oggi* (Florence, 1972), p. 127.
31. Moro, p. 75.
32. Betti, *Teatro completo*, p. 534.

33. *Ibid.*
34. *Ibid.*, p. 538.
35. *Ibid.*, p. 539.
36. *Ibid.*
37. *Ibid.*, p. 533.
38. *Ibid.*, p. 530. Eugene O'Neill had used this device in *Strange Interlude* (1926).
39. *Ibid.*, p. 559.
40. *Ibid.*, p. 561.
41. *Ibid.*, p. 559.
42. *Ibid.*
43. *Ibid.*, p. 563.
44. *Ibid.*, p. 565.
45. Franco Musarra, *Impegno e astrazione nell'opera di Ugo Betti* (L'Aquila, 1974), p. 42.
46. Betti, *Teatro completo*, p. 569.
47. *Ibid.*, p. 577.
48. *Ibid.*
49. Di Pietro, II, 188.
50. Moro, p. 73.
51. *Ibid.*, p. 80.
52. Betti, *Teatro completo*, p. 841.
53. *Ibid.*, p. 839.
54. *Ibid.*, p. 808.
55. *Ibid.*, p. 845.
56. Di Pietro, II, 195.
57. *Ibid.*
58. Mario Apollonio, "Ricordo di Ugo Betti e linee di una possible ricognizione," *Drammaturgia* (Summer, 1954), p. 78.
59. Di Pietro, II, 205.
60. Cologni, p. 95.
61. Gino Rizzo, "Regression-Progression in Ugo Betti's Drama," *cit.*, p. 114.
62. Silvio D'Amico, Introduzione to Ugo Betti, *Teatro completo*, p. 11.
63. Luigi Pirandello, *Naked Masks* (New York, 1952), p. 363.
64. D'Amico, p. 12.
65. Torresani, pp. 80–81.
66. De Sanctis, p. 270.
67. *Ibid.*, p. 271.
68. Di Pietro, II, 198.
69. *Ibid.*

70. Betti, *Teatro completo*, p. 919.

71. Moro, p. 81, n. 13.

72. Betti, *Teatro completo*, p. 905.

73. *Ibid.*

74. *Ibid.*, p. 920.

75. *Ibid.*, p. 922.

76. *Ibid.*, p. 923.

77. *Ibid.*, p. 944.

78. *Ibid.*, p. 945.

79. *Ibid.*

80. *Ibid.*, p. 947.

81. *Ibid.*, p. 950.

82. *Ibid.*, pp. 951–952.

83. *Ibid.*

84. See note 56 of Chapter 2.

85. Betti, *Teatro completo*, p. 954.

86. *Ibid.*, pp. 957–958.

87. *Ibid.*, p. 958.

88. *Ibid.*

89. *Ibid.*

90. Ottavio Spadaro, "Ugo Betti o del terzo atto," *Sipario*, V, 48 (1950), p. 17.

91. Di Pietro, II, 216.

92. *Ibid.*

93. It is Betti's word. Di Pietro, II, 216.

94. G.M. Guglielmino, as quoted by Cologni, *cit.*, 107.

95. Moro, p. 87.

96. D'Amico, p. 11. The critic uses these words in a different context.

97. Gino Rizzo, Introduction to *Ugo Betti: Three Plays* (New York, 1966), p. xvi.

98. Betti, *The Inquiry*, trans. by David Gullette and Gino Rizzo, in *Ugo Betti: Three Plays, cit.*, p. 3.

99. Betti's word. Di Pietro, II, 216. For the preceding quotation see note 38, Chapter 2.

100. D'Amico, p. 13.

101. Ottavio Spadaro, in Cologni, *cit.*, p. 107.

102. Betti, *The Inquiry*, p. 4.

103. *Ibid.*, p. 5.

104. Fiocco, p. 28.

105. Betti, *The Inquiry*, pp. 6–7.

106. *Ibid.*, p. 6.

107. *Ibid.*, p. 9.
108. *Ibid.*, p. 10.
109. *Ibid.*, p. 13.
110. *Ibid.*, p. 16.
111. *Ibid.*, p. 18.
112. *Ibid.*, p. 21.
113. *Ibid.*, p. 25.
114. *Ibid.*, p. 6.
115. *Ibid.*, p. 8.
116. *Ibid.*
117. *Ibid.*, p. 11.
118. *Ibid.*, p. 15.
119. *Ibid.*, p. 18.
120. *Ibid.*, p. 24.
121. *Ibid.*, p. 29.
122. *Ibid.*, p. 31.
123. *Ibid.*, p. 37.
124. *Ibid.*, p. 38.
125. *Ibid.*, p. 39.
126. *Ibid.*, pp. 39–40.
127. Pirandello, pp. 222, 228, 230.
128. Betti, *The Inquiry*, p. 41.
129. *Ibid.*, p. 42.
130. *Ibid.*, p. 45.
131. *Ibid.*, p. 46.
132. *Ibid.*, p. 51.
133. *Ibid.*, p. 52.
134. *Ibid.*, p. 55.
135. *Ibid.*
136. *Ibid.*, p. 45.
137. *Ibid.*, p. 56.
138. *Ibid.*, p. 58.
139. *Ibid.*, p. 59.
140. *Ibid.*, p. 60.
141. *Ibid.*, p. 63.
142. *Ibid.*
143. *Ibid.*, p. 64.
144. *Ibid.*, p. 69.
145. *Ibid.*, p. 70.
146. *Ibid.*
147. *Ibid.*, p. 71.
148. *Ibid.*, p. 17.

149. *Ibid.*, pp. 22, 30, 31, 38, 58.

150. *Ibid.*, p. 24.

151. *Ibid.*, p. 38.

152. Giorgio Pullini, *Cinquant'anni di teatro italiano* (Bologna, 1960), p. 93.

153. Betti, *The Inquiry*, p. 71.

154. Torresani, p. 86.

155. D'Amico, as quoted by Torresani, *cit.*, p. 86.

156. J.A. Scott, "The Message of Ugo Betti," *Italica*, XXXVII, 1 (1960), p. 44.

157. *Ibid*, p. 45.

158. Translated with this titled by Henry Reed (San Francisco, 1961).

159. Translated with this title by Gino Rizzo and David Gullette, in *Ugo Betti: Three Plays*, *cit*. We will quote from this translation.

160. Di Pietro, II, 223–224, n. 3.

161. *Ibid.*, p. 224.

162. McWilliam, Introduction, cit., p. XIV.

163. Betti, *The Inquiry*, p. 11.

164. Betti, *Goat Island*, p. 108.

165. *Ibid.*, pp. 93–94.

166. Di Pietro, II, 225.

167. Humphrey D.F. Kitto, *Form and Meaning in Drama* (London, 1959), p. 231.

168. *Ibid.*

169. Betti, *Goat Island*, p. 130.

170. *Ibid.*, p. 86.

171. *Ibid.*, p. 90.

172. *Ibid.*, p. 89.

173. *Ibid.*, p. 90.

174. *Ibid.*, p. 84.

175. *Ibid.*, p. 114.

176. *Ibid.*

177. *Ibid.*, p. 107.

178. *Ibid.*, p. 109.

179. *Ibid.*, p. 113.

180. *Ibid.*, p. 130.

181. *Ibid.*

182. *Ibid.*, p. 91.

183. *Ibid.*, pp. 130–131.

184. *Ibid.*, p. 129.

185. *Ibid.*, p. 126.

186. Di Pietro, II, 225.
187. Betti, *Goat Island*, p. 120.
188. De Sanctis, p. 250.
189. W.H. Auden, "The Christian Tragic Hero," in *Moderns on Tragedy*, ed. by Lionel Abel (New York, 1967), p. 40.
190. *Ibid.*
191. Betti, *Goat Island*, p. 133.
192. D'Amico, p. 14.
193. V. Talarico, as reported by Moro, *cit.*, p. 162.
194. E. Contini, as reported by Moro, *Ibid.*
195. See Cologni, pp. 110–113.
196. Moro, p. 92.
197. Jean Neveux, as reported by Cologni, *cit.*, pp. 108–109.

Chapter 5

1. Di Pietro, II, 239.
2. McWilliam, Introduction, p. xiv.
3. Betti, *Struggle Till Dawn*, trans, by G.H. McWilliam, *cit.*, p. 64.
4. *Ibid.*
5. *Ibid.*, p. 69.
6. *Ibid.*, p. 71.
7. *Ibid.*, p. 73.
8. *Ibid.*, p. 77.
9. Moro, p. 96.
10. Betti, *Struggle Till Dawn*, p. 84.
11. *Ibid.*, p. 87.
12. *Ibid.*, p. 92.
13. Di Pietro, II, 240.
14. Gildo Moro regards this scene as weak. Moro, *cit.*, p. 94.
15. McWilliam, Introduction, p. xiii.
16. Betti, *Struggle Till Dawn*, pp. 118–119.
17. Torresani, p. 90.
18. Cologni, p. 119.
19. Torresani, p. 91.
20. Fiocco, p. 33.
21. Harold Clurman, in a review of the play's performance, with the adapted title *Time of Vengeance*, in London, *The Nation* (Jan. 2, 1960), p. 19.
22. Betti, *Teatro completo*, p. 694.

23. *Ibid.*, p. 695.
24. *Ibid.*
25. *Ibid.*, p. 713.
26. *Ibid.*, p. 725.
27. Maurice Clavel, "Irène sauvée," *Cahiers de la compagnie Renaud-Barrault*, 7 (1954), as quoted by Cologni, *cit.*, p. 120.
28. We are using Vladimir Propp's terminology from *Morphology of the Folk Tale* (Bloomington, Ind., 1958).
29. Betti, *Teatro completo*, p. 737.
30. *Ibid.*, p. 740.
31. Di Pietro, II, 249.
32. Jacobbi, p. 137.
33. Di Pietro, II, 243.
34. *Ibid.*, p. 250.
35. Torresani, p. 92.
36. Giovanni Calendoli, as quoted by Cologni, *cit.*, p. 122.
37. Betti, *Teatro completo*, p. 1113.
38. Moro, p. 112.
39. Betti, *Teatro completo*, p. 1127.
40. *Ibid.*, p. 1141.
41. *Ibid.*, p. 1146.
42. *Ibid.*, pp. 1146–1147.
43. *Ibid.*, p. 1146.
44. *Ibid.*, p. 1147.
45. *Ibid.*
46. *Ibid.*, p. 1148.
47. *Ibid.*, p. 1149.
48. *Ibid.*, p. 1150.
49. *Ibid.*, p. 1155.
50. *Ibid.*, p. 1157.
51. *Ibid.*
52. *Ibid.*, p. 1159.
53. *Ibid.*, p. 1161.
54. *Ibid.*, p. 1162.
55. *Ibid.*
56. *Ibid.*, p. 1163.
57. *Ibid.*
58. *Ibid.*, p. 1164.
59. *Ibid.*
60. See Moro, p. 168.
61. Cologni, p. 121.
62. See Moro, p. 169.

63. *Ibid.*, p. 168.

64. Jacobbi, p. 140.

65. *Ibid.*

66. J.-P. Sartre, *Saint Genet, Actor and Martyr* (New York, 1963), p. 344. These remarks on *The Queen and the Rebels* were published in Emanuele Licastro, "Beyond Politics: Betti's Two Political Plays," *Rivista di Studi Italiani* (Toronto), 1 (1983).

67. That is, man in his unembellished reality: hence such a statement as "a rose has no other duty than to look as little as possible like an artichoke." But Walter Kerr, writing in *The New York Times* of a Broadway production of *The Queen and the Rebels* with Colleen Dewhurst, was overly anxious to label it "pontifically philosophical." (*The New York Times*, Oct. 10, 1982, Sect. 2, p. 3).

68. John Gatt-Rutter, *Writers & Politics in Modern Italy* (New York, 1974), p. 20.

69. Both Walter Kerr (*The New York Times, Ibid.*) and Brendan Gill, the reviewer for *The New Yorker* (*The New Yorker*, Oct. 11, 1982), writing of the aforementioned production of *The Queen and the Rebels* (see note 67) mistake this unidentifiableness as a lack of political realism rather than viewing it as an attempt to redirect the order of the play's outward political theme into a more universal one. Another critic, E. Martin Browne, states that Betti "clearly prefers to liberate himself from place in the geographical sense—his plays are set in an atmosphere of the mind expressed by a place unlocalized except in so far as the play's story demands it. [*The Queen and the Rebels*], with its mysterious room on a frontier showing only the characteristics of troubled times, is a good example though less extreme than most." Introduction to *Three European Plays* (London, 1965), p. 9.

70. Betti, *The Queen and the Rebels*, trans. by Henry Reed, in *Three Plays by Ugo Betti, cit.*, p. 31.

71. *Ibid.*, pp. 31–32.

72. *Ibid.*, p. 33.

73. *Ibid.*, p. 35.

74. *Ibid.*, pp. 43–44.

75. *Ibid.*, p. 29.

76. *Ibid.*, p. 35.

77. *Ibid.*, p. 60.

78. *Ibid.*, p. 42.

79. *Ibid.*, p. 55.

80. *Ibid.*, p. 72.

81. *Ibid.*, p. 82.

82. *Ibid.*, p. 93.

83. *Ibid.*

84. *Ibid.*, p. 96.

85. And certainly not revolutionaries in particular. Both W. Kerr and B. Gill (see notes 67 and 69) lament that without a specified place the characters are not revolutionaries of any specific kind, but this is exactly Betti's intention. His revolutionaries are not specific but special. They face the Dostoyescan "stone wall."

86. Lucienne Portier, "Le Théâtre en question: Ugo Betti," Italianistica, 2 (1973), p. 255.

87. Alessandro Blasetti, "Un invito al riscatto," *Sipario*, VI, 61 (1951), p. 40.

88. Brooks Atkinson, "The Problem of Betti," *The New York Times* (Dec. 27, 1959), sect. 2, p. 1.

89. Jean Anouilh, as quoted by Moro, *cit.*, p. 167.

90. Brooks Atkinson, in a review of the play's performance, *The New York Times* (Oct. 14, 1952), p. 40. The play was adapted by Alfred Drake, who starred in the title role, and Edward Eager.

91. Walcott Gibbs, in a review of the same performance, *The New Yorker* (Oct. 25, 1952), p. 72.

92. Atkinson, "The Problem of Betti," *cit.*, *Ibid.*

93. Di Pietro, II, p. 267.

94. *Ibid.*

95. Cologni, p. 139.

96. *Ibid.*

97. Betti, *The Gambler*, trans. by Barbara Kennedy, in *Ugo Betti: Three Plays*, *cit.*, p. 141.

98. *Ibid.*, p. 163.

99. *Ibid.*

100. *Ibid.*, p. 165.

101. *Ibid.*, pp. 165–166.

102. *Ibid.*, p. 181.

103. *Ibid.*, p. 185.

104. *Ibid.*, p. 195.

105. *Ibid.*, pp. 199–200.

106. *Ibid.*, p. 201.

107. *Ibid.*, p. 202.

108. As reported by Calendoli, *cit.*, p. 137.

109. Moro, p. 107.

110. Atkinson, in his review, *cit.*

111. These observations on *The Burnt Flower-Bed* were first published in Emanuele Licastro, "Beyond Politics: Betti's Two Political Plays," *Ibid.*

112. Betti, *The Burnt Flower-Bed*, trans. by Henry Reed, in *Three Plays by Ugo Betti, cit.*, p. 136.

113. *Ibid.*, p. 137.

114. *Ibid.*, p. 139.

115. *Ibid.*, p. 140.

116. *Ibid.*, p. 141.

117. *Ibid.*, p. 143.

118. *Ibid.*, p. 142.

119. See note 85.

120. Moro, p. 112.

121. Betti, *The Burnt Flower-Bed*, p. 150.

122. *Ibid.*, p. 151.

123. *Ibid.*, p. 156.

124. *Ibid.*, p. 166.

125. *Ibid.*, p. 176.

126. *Ibid.*

127. *Ibid.*, pp. 177–178.

128. *Ibid.*, p. 178.

129. *Ibid.*, p. 179.

130. *Ibid.*, p. 181.

131. *Ibid.*

132. *Ibid.*

133. *Ibid.*, p. 185.

134. *Ibid.*, p. 183.

135. *Ibid.*, p. 185.

136. *Ibid.*, p. 186.

137. Betti, *Teatro completo*, p. 1217.

138. Betti, *The Fugitive*, p. 123.

139. *Ibid.*, p. 165.

140. *Ibid.*, p. 163.

141. *Ibid.*, p. 144.

142. See Susan Sontag, *Illness as Metaphor* (New York, 1978).

143. Betti, *The Fugitive*, p. 164.

144. *Ibid.*, p. 138.

145. *Ibid.*, p. 141.

146. *Ibid.*, p. 181.

147. Betti, *Teatro completo*, p. 1163.

148. Betti, *The Fugitive*, p. 134.

149. *Ibid.*, p. 139.

150. *Ibid.*, p. 143.

151. *Ibid.*, p. 165.

152. *Ibid.*, p. 179.

153. *Ibid.*, p. 180.

154. *Ibid.*, p. 181.

155. *Ibid.*, p. 183.

156. *Ibid.*, p. 166.

157. George Steiner, *The Death of Tragedy* (New York, 1963), p. 8.

158. John Gassner, *Masters of the Drama* (New York, 1954), p. 445.

159. Ugo Betti, *Il diritto e la rivoluzione*, in *Scritti inediti* (Bari, 1964), p. 99.

Chapter 6

1. Musarra, p. 53.

2. Lilana A. Luzzani, "Ugo Betti poeta," *Realismo lirico*, 82–88 (Sept. 1967–Oct. 1968), p. 123.

3. Alfredo Galletti speaks of "melodic invention," *Il Novecento* (Milan, 1954), p. 555.

4. Musarra, p. 51.

5. Betti in his notes, as reported by Di Pietro, I, 149–150.

6. Adriano Tilgher, as quoted by Di Pietro, II, 79, n. 2.

7. Barbetti, p. 46.

8. Ugo Betti, *Poesie* (Bologna, 1957), p. 133.

9. *Ibid.*, p. 134.

10. Luzzani, p. 124.

11. Betti, p. 144.

12. *Ibid.*, the poem *Calore* (*Warmth*), p. 121.

13. *Ibid.*, p. 161. We may view these two scenes as primal in a phylogenetic sense. Years later, Cust, the protagonist of *Corruption in the Palace of Justice* remembers having witnessed, as a child, his father and mother mating. See p. 113.

14. Di Pietro, II, 118.

15. Betti, *Poesie*, p. 184.

Chapter 7

1. Di Pietro, I, 91.

2. Ugo Betti, *Caino* (Milan, 1928), p. 177.

3. Di Pietro, I, 86.

4. Betti, *Caino*, p. 203.

5. *Ibid.*, p. 207.

6. Ugo Betti, *Raccolta di novelle*, ed. by Lia Fava (Bologna, 1963), p. 158.

7. *Ibid.*, p. 159.

8. *Ibid.*, p. 160.

9. Arnaldo Boccelli, "Scrittori d'oggi," *Nuova Antologia*, 1449 (Aug, 1932), p. 275.

10. Betti, *Poesie*, p. 119.

11. Betti, as reported by Di Pietro, II, 36, n. 1.

12. Betti, *Raccolta di novelle*, p. 136.

13. Boccelli, "Scrittori d'oggi," *Nuova Antologia*, 1473, (Aug., 1933), p. 465.

14. Betti, *Raccolta di novelle*, p. 172.

15. *Ibid.*

16. *Ibid.*, p. 138.

17. *Ibid.*

18. *Ibid.*, p. 180.

19. *Ibid.*, pp. 186–187.

20. Di Pietro, II, 163.

21. Ugo Betti, *Una strana serata* (Milan, 1948), p. 161.

22. Di Pietro, II, 164.

23. Betti, *Una strana serata*, p. 76.

24. *Ibid.*, p. 37.

25. *Ibid.*, p. 111.

26. *Ibid.*, p. 114.

27. Ugo Betti, *La piera alta* (Milan, 1948), pp. 3, 10, 16.

28. *Ibid.*, p. 12.

29. *Ibid.*, p. 43.

30. *Ibid.*, p. 120.

31. *Ibid.*, pp. 143–144.

32. *Ibid.*, p. 160.

33. Betti, *Il diritto e la rivoluzione*, p. 96.

34. *Ibid.*, pp. 96–97.

35. *Ibid.*, p. 82.

36. Betti, "Religion and the Theatre," p. 11.

37. *Ibid.*

Bibliography

Primary Sources

Le nozze di Teti e Peleo. Camerino: Savini, 1910. A translation into blank verse of Catullus' *Epithalamion of Thetis and Peleus*.

Considerazioni sulla forza maggiore come limite di responsabilità del vettore ferroviario. Camerino: Tonnarelli, 1920. An essay on how to distribute responsibility in case of a railroad accident.

Il Re pensieroso. Naples: Treves, 1922. A book of verse.

Caino. Milan: Corbaccio, 1928. A book of short stories.

Canzonette — La morte. Milan: Mondadori, 1932. A book of verse.

Le case. Milan: Mondadori, 1933. A book of short stories.

Uomo e donna. Milan: Mondadori, 1937. A book of verse.

Una strana serata. Milan: Garzanti, 1944. A book of short stories.

La piera alta. Milan: Garzanti, 1948. A novel elaborated from a movie script.

Teatro. Bologna: Cappelli, 1955. A collection of Betti's plays up to 1950, with a Preface by Silvio D'Amico.

Teatro postumo. Bologna: Cappelli, 1955. Betti's last three plays, with a Preface by Achille Fiocco.

Poesie. Bologna: Cappelli, 1957. Contains the three books of poetry previously published and the new *Ultime liriche (1938-1953)*.

Teatro completo. Bologna: Cappelli, 1971. Contains the two preceding volumes of plays.

Religione e teatro. Brescia: Morcelliana, 1957. A critical essay on religion and the theater, and another on the 29th canto of *Paradise*, with a Foreword by his wife.

Scritti inediti. Edited by Antonio Di Pietro. Bari: "Centro Librario," 1964. Betti's doctoral dissertation, *Il diritto e la rivoluzione*; some unpublished poems; *La Donna sullo scudo*, "Legend in Three Acts" in verse, written in collaboration with Osvaldo Gibertini, journalist and author of minor theater pieces; the movie script *I tre del pra' di sopra*; a verse version of the play *L'isola meravigliosa*, written as a libretto; the short story *Quelli del padiglione*, Betti's last fiction.

Raccolta di novelle. Edited with Introduction by Lia Fava. Bologna: Cappelli, 1963. A selection from Betti's three books of short stories plus eight more published in various periodicals from 1932 to 1952.

Two Plays, Frana allo Scalo Nord, L'aiuola bruciata. Edited with Introduction, notes, and vocabulary by G.H. McWilliam. Manchester: University Press, 1965 (reprinted in 1968, 1973, 1978). A book for English-speaking college students of Italian. The Introduction, in English, is most lucidly argued.

Novelle. Edited with Introduction and notes by Mario Ortolani. San Severino, Marche: Varano, 1968. A selection of stories for high school students, each with an introductory note.

Three Plays by Ugo Betti. Translated, and with Foreword, by Henry Reed. London: Gollancz, 1956. Later, New York: Grove Press, 1958. The plays are *La Regina e gli Insorti, L'aiuola bruciata*, and *Il paese delle vacanze*.

Crime on Goat Island. Translated by Henry Reed, with an Introduction by G.H. McWilliam. San Francisco: Chandler Publishing Co., 1961. Translation of *Delitto all'Isola delle capre*. The Introduction is excellent.

Corruption in the Palace of Justice. Translated by Henry Reed. In Robert W. Corrigan, ed., *The New Theatre of Europe*. Vol. 1. New York: Dell Publishing Co., 1962.

Three Plays on Justice. Translated, with an Introduction by G.H. McWilliam. San Francisco, Chandler Publishing Co., 1964. The plays are *Frana allo Scalo Nord, Lotta fino all'alba*, and *La fuggitiva*. McWilliam's introductory comments are very thoughtful.

The Queen and the Rebels. Translated by Henry Reed. In *Three European Plays*. Edited and introduced by E. Martin Browne. London: Penguin Book, 1965. (The other two plays are: Jean Anouilh, *Ring Round the Moon*, trans. by Christopher Fry and Jean-Paul Sartre, *In Camera*, trans. by Stuart Gilbert.)

Corruption in the Palace of Justice. Translated by Henry Reed. In Alvin Kernan, ed., *Classics of Modern Theater.* New York: Harcourt, Brace and World, 1965.

Ugo Betti: Three Plays. With Introduction by Gino Rizzo. New York: Hill and Wang, 1966. The plays are *Ispezione*, translated by David Gullette and Gino Rizzo, *Delitto all'Isola delle Capre*, translated by Gino Rizzo and David Gullette, and *Il giocatore*, translated by Barbara Kennedy. A most learned and insightful Introduction.

Crime on Goat Island. Translated by Henry Reed. In Robert Corrigan, ed., *Masterpieces of the Modern Italian Theatre.* New York: Collier Books, 1967.

"Religion and the Theatre." Translated by Gino Rizzo and William Meriwether. *The Tulane Drama Review*, V (Dec. 1960) 3–12. Also in *Theatre in the Twentieth Century.* Edited by Robert W. Corrigan. Freeport, N.Y.: Grove Press, 1963. Pp. 114–124. Translation of "Religione e teatro."

"Preface to *The Mistress.*" Translated by Gino Rizzo and William Meriwether. *The Tulane Drama Review*, V (Dec. 1960), 13–14. Translation of Betti's Preface to his first play, *La padrona.*

"Essays, Correspondence, Notes." Selected and translated by William Meriwether and Gino Rizzo. *The Tulane Drama Review*, VIII (Spring 1964), 51–86. Contains some short critical essays written for various periodicals; some letters dealing with Betti's art and his concern for recognition; the notes he wrote before and during the composition of *Corruption in the Palace of Justice* and *Crime on Goat Island.*

Secondary Sources

BOOKS

Alessio, Antonio. *Ugo Betti.* Genoa: Di Stefano, 1963. A volume divided into critical analysis and a selection of passages from Betti's *oeuvre* which argues the critic's point of view. For Alessio Betti deals mainly with man as a metaphysical entity. Alessio indicates Betti's use of images from nature.

Barbetti, Emilio. *Il teatro di Ugo Betti.* Florence: La Nuova Italia, 1943. The first book on Betti. It covers half his *oeuvre*, and although some pages are uncritical, there are many penetrating insights nonetheless. Barbetti is also interesting on the poetry and short stories.

Cologni, Franco. *La fortuna del teatro di Ugo Betti*. Brescia: Morcelliana, 1959. An invaluable volume for its large and accurate bibliography on Betti up to 1958.

_____. *Ugo Betti*. Bologna: Capelli, 1960. After a first chapter on the poetry, wherein Cologni finds the origin of many theatrical themes, he analyzes the plays. He quotes many critical remarks about the plays and the opinions of reviewers at the premières, and lists the various acting companies and casts.

Curetti, Elettra. *Zu den Dramen von Ugo Betti*. Zurich: Juris Druck, 1966. The critic sees Betti's *oeuvre* as a depiction of man's *iter* to God. She perceives Betti's world as one of "transcendental realism," where time and space are not important.

De Michelis, Eurialo. *La poesia di Ugo Betti*. Florence: La Nuova Italia, n.d. Written about 1936, it is the most extensive study of Betti's poetry, although De Michelis exaggerates his achievements. He even though Betti was "the greatest poet of the generation of D'Annunzio."

Di Pietro, Antonio. *L'opera di Ugo Betti*. 2 vols. Bari: "Centro Librario," 1908. Two most useful volumes for detailed biographical and literary information about Betti's life, the history of his works and their publication. Di Pietro makes wide use of the extensive notes Betti wrote before and during the compositions of his plays. Informed and on the main a good critical analysis.

Fiocco, Achille. *Ugo Betti*. Rome: De Luca, 1954. Fiocco briefly comments on each play, but these comments, with a few exceptions are without real depth. At times his moralistic approach prevents an accurate assessment of Betti's intent. For example, he accuses Betti of "physiological fatalism" in *Crime on Goat Island*.

Moro, Gildo. *Il teatro di Ugo Betti*. Milan: Marzorati, 1973. Starts with a chapter on Betti's themes, and then considers the development of these themes in the *oeuvre*. The last chapter is on the history of the plays' performances and the reaction of the public and critics. Supplements the aforementioned volume by Cologni.

Musarra, Franco. *Impegno e astrazione nell'opera di Ugo Betti.* L'Aquila: L.U. Japadre, 1974. The author argues that home, emigration, and war are Betti's principal points of departure for the composition of his plays. He perceives three phases in Betti's poetic: man as a member of society, as an individual, and as a religious entity. For Musarra the most accomplished plays are those in which these three concerns are well balanced.

Pellecchia, Gioacchino. *Saggio sul teatro di Ugo Betti.* Naples: Istituto Editoriale del Mezzogiorno, 1963. This critic extrapolates the themes of justice, good and evil, innocence, love, and sacrifice from Betti's plays. Pellecchia, perhaps too consistently, reads the plays from a Christian point of view.

ARTICLES AND CHAPTERS

Apollonio, Carla. "Ugo Betti." *Letteratura italiana. I Contemporanei.* Milan: Marzorati, 1963. Vol. II, 1021–1036. A general introduction.

Apollonio, Mario. "Ugo Betti," *Letteratura dei contemporanei.* Brescia: La Scuola, 1956. Pp. 555–559. Brief but acute observations on Betti.

Barbetti, Emilio. "Statura di Ugo Betti," *Il Ponte,* XII (1954), 1924–1935. Perhaps the most knowledgeable critic on Betti at the time of this essay, Barbetti tries to place him in historical perspective.

Curato, Baldo. "Betti, o della Poesia," *Sessant'anni di teatro in Italia.* Milan: Denti, 1947. Pp. 317–353. A good reading of some of the plays but some analyses are unconvincing.

De Sanctis, G.B. "Due saggi sul Betti. I. Senso della crisi in Ugo Betti II. Betti tra favola e realismo," *Studi sul teatro.* Ravenna: Longo, 1968. Pp. 225–274. One essay deals with alienation in Betti, the other with realism and fable in his theater.

Doglio, Federico. Preface to *Corruzione al Palazzo di Giustizia.* Bologna: Cappelli, 1966. Pp. 5–19. A general introduction to Betti with some insightful comments on *Corruption in the Palace of Justice.*

Fiocco, Achille. "L'heritage de Pirandello," *World Theater*, III (1954), 24–30. Fiocco writes, in part, about Pirandello's influence on Betti.

Gatt-Rutter, John. "Ugo Betti: The Whore as Queen," *Writers & Politics in Modern Italy*. New York: Holmes & Meier, 1974. Pp. 17–21. Gott-Rutter reads Betti through the narrow perspective of politics. Some of his thoughts are interesting, although he reads the verdict of compassion at the end of *Landslide* as justifying a "political, social and economic system."

Genot, Gerard. "Ugo Betti, L'Engrenage et la balance," *La mort de Godot*. Essays edited and presented by Pierre Brunel. Paris: Lettres Modernes Minard, 1970. Pp. 75–112. Genot argues that Betti's vision should be perceived "only through the nuances of his dramatic treatment." With some valuable commentary about Betti's theater.

Illiano, Antonio. "Ugo Betti's Last Plays," *Perspectives on Contemporary Literature*, I, 1 (1975), 22–30. Brief but thoughtful essay. It states that "Betti's mysticism stems from what may be called a human [not humanistic] immanence of the idea of God," and that "his preaching is a way of confessing his own unfulfilled need to believe."

Jacobbi, Ruggero. "Ugo Betti nel paese degli angeli," *Teatro da ieri a domani*. Florence: La Nuova Italia, 1972. Pp. 115–143. Particularly insightful on *Irene innocente*, *Husband and Wife*, *The Duck Hunter*, and *Struggle Till Dawn*.

Licastro, Emanuele. "Deragliamenti in *Frana allo Scalo Nord*," *NEMLA Italian Studies*, V (1981), 89–97. It shows how *Landslide* moves from sociological to psychological and then to ontological concerns. It analyzes Bettian theatrical techniques.

_____. "Beyond Politics: Betti's Two Political Plays," *Rivista di Studi Italiani*, I (1983), 147–158. An analysis of *The Queen and the Rebels* and *The Burnt Flower-Bed*. It asserts that Betti is finally not interested in politics *per se* but in ultimate questions.

Lucignani, Luciano. "Engagement et disponibilité dans le théâtre italien contemporain," *Le théâtre Modern. Hommes et tendances*. Ed. by Jean Jacquot. Paris: Editions cu centre National de la

Recherche Scientifique, 1958. Pp. 309–320. Betti's theater is seen as an expression of a conservative ideology interested in maintaining the *status quo*.

MacClintock, Lander. "Ugo Betti," *Modern Language Journal*, XXXV (1951), 251–257. MacClintock remains unconvinced by Betti's theater.

McWilliam, G.B. "Interpreting Betti," *The Tulane Drama Review*, V (Dec., 1960), 15–23. A penetrating essay on how to perform Betti's plays.

_____. "The Minor Plays of Ugo Betti," *Italian Studies*, XX (1965), 78–107. An excellent analysis of *The Marvelous Island*, *The Flood*, and Betti's four comedies.

_____. "Pirandello e Betti," *Atti del congresso internazionale di studi pirandelliani*. Florence: Le Monnier, 1967. Pp. 519–536. McWilliam draws revealing parallels between Pirandello and Betti.

Pandolfi, Vito. "Italian Theatre Since the War," *The Tulane Drama Review*, VIII (Spring 1964), 87–100. In three pages devoted to Betti, Pandolfi argues that his ideas are those "on which our society depends to sublimate its guilt." Pandolfi uses a kind of socio-economic approach.

Portier, Lucienne. "Le théâtre en question: Ugo Betti." *Italianistica*, II (1973), 249–267. Thought-provoking; Portier thinks Betti is too committed to mankind to become seriously involved in the "particular and passing event[s]" of the politics of his time.

Rizzo, Gino. "Regression-Progression in Ugo Betti's Drama," *The Tulane Drama Review*, VIII (Fall 1963), 101–129. Rizzo argues intelligently that Betti's characters are torn between a "retrogressive movement" toward childhood and the "forward movement of life."

Scott, J.A. "The Message of Ugo Betti," *Italica*, XXXVII (March 1960), 44–57. An emotional analysis of *The Inquiry*, *The Queen and the Rebels*, and *The Burnt Flower-Bed*.

Torresani, Sergio. "Ugo Betti," *Il teatro italiano negli ultimi vent'anni*

(1945-1965). Cremona: Gianni Mangiarotti, 1965. Pp. 57–102. A good commentary on Betti's plays.

Usmiani, Renate. "Twentieth-century Man, the Guilt-Ridden Animal," *Mosaic*, III (Summer 1970), 163–178. A keen analysis of the "kinship between Kafka on the one hand and Betti and Dürrenmatt on the other."

————. "The 'Felix Culpa' Motif in the Drama of Ugo Betti," *Humanities Association of Canada, Bulletin*, XXI (Winter 1970), 39–44. Usmiani analyses *Landslide, Corruption in the Palace of Justice,* and *The Gambler*, arguing Betti's "gradual evolution of religious awareness."

Index

Published translations of Betti's works are cited in italics

171